THE REIGN OF GOD IS IN YOUR MIDST

THE REIGN
OF GOD
IS IN YOUR
MIDST

PRAYING

THE GOSPEL

OF LUKE

DONALD E. COLLINS

UPPER
ROOM BOOKS
NASHVILLE

THE REIGN OF GOD IS IN YOUR MIDST

Scripture quotations designated TEV are from the *Good News Bible, The Bible in Today's English Version,* copyright by American Bible Society 1966, 1971, © 1976, and are used by permission.

Scripture quotations designated NRSV are from the New Revised Standard Version of the Bible, copyright 1989 by the Division of Christian Education, National Council of the Churches of Christ in the United States of America, and are used by permission.

Scripture quotations designated RSV are from the Revised Standard Version of the Bible, copyright 1946, 1952, and © 1971 by the Division of Christian Education, National Council of the Churches of Christ in the United States of America, and are used by permission.

Scripture quotations designated NEB are from the *New English Bible,* © The Delegates of the Oxford University Press and the Syndics of the Cambridge University Press 1961 and 1970, and are reprinted by permission.

Scripture quotations designated NAB are from the New American Bible, copyright © 1970, by the Confraternity of Christian Doctrine, Washington, D.C. Used by permission of the copyright holder. All rights reserved.

Scripture quotations designated JB are taken from the *Jerusalem Bible,* published and copyright © 1966, 1967, and 1968 by Darton, Longman & Todd Ltd and Doubleday & Co. Inc., and are used by permission of the publishers.

Scripture quotations identified CEV are from the Contemporary English Version text. Copyright © American Bible Society 1991, 1992. Used by permission.

Any scripture quotation designated AP is the author's paraphrase.

Excerpt from "God of Grace and God of Glory" © 1930 Harry Emerson Fosdick used by permission of Elinor Fosdick Downs.

Haiku poetry by Kathrine Laycock used by permission of the author.

Cover Design: Bruce Gore/Gore Studio
Cover Photograph: © Adamsmith Productions/Westlight
First Printing: March 1993 (5)
ISBN 0-8358-0675-8
Library of Congress Catalog Card Number: 92-61440

Printed in the United States of America

CONTENTS

THE JOURNEY TO JERUSALEM (9:51–19:27)

PREFACE

CHRISTIANS IN OUR TIME are often surprised to discover that their spiritual ancestors include many in the fourth century who reacted to the pagan culture around them by abandoning relative comforts and familiar surroundings in order to find salvation alone in the desert. The result was a blossoming of religious vitality in which countless others traveled great distances to seek the spiritual counsel of these "desert fathers and mothers."

In recent decades some have seen a parallel of sorts in our own quest for ways to survive the stresses and strains of life in the twentieth century. It is a loose parallel to be sure. Lacking the patience of those in the fourth century, we are more likely to settle for instant answers and temporary solutions. In our modern search for "salvation," we and our contemporaries have often turned to secular rather than sacred resources. These have included the human potential movement, psychotherapy, transcendental meditation, second homes, exotic vacations, alcohol and other drugs, cult groups, and throw-away relationships.

Among those who understand that such solutions are shallow at best, there is often a hungering for something more. While that hungering may be difficult to articulate, most of us are well aware that what we yearn for is a genuine experience of the holy in our everyday lives. We are not alone in such yearnings. Our spiritual ancestors have been there before us:

> O God, you are my God,
> and I long for you.
> My whole being desires you;
> like a dry, worn-out,
> and waterless land,
> my soul is thirsty for you.
>   (Psalm 63:1, TEV)

As a deer longs for flowing streams,
so my soul longs for you, O God.
(Psalm 42:1, NRSV)

And as Isaiah pointed out, God is ready to meet our need:

The Lord says,
   "Come, everyone who is thirsty—
      here is water!
. . . Listen to me and do what I say,
and you will enjoy the best food of all."
(Isaiah 55:1a, 2c, TEV)

This book is an invitation to join with those who have gone before us, not just to read scripture with our eyes and hear it with our ears, but to pray it with our hearts! More specifically, it is an invitation to find new life in Christ by praying the Gospel According to Luke.

In the chapter, "An Invitation to Luke's Gospel," I have tried to outline some of the characteristics that make the third Gospel my own favorite as well as my choice for the meditations offered in this book. It is, as Luke says in his own preface, "an orderly account." There is a clear interest in prayer and in Jesus as a person of prayer. Luke's commitment to the prophetic tradition is evident both in the magnificent canticles of Mary and Zechariah and in the Isaiah passage read by Jesus in Nazareth as a paradigm for his own ministry. This prophetic interest is present, not only in Luke's special emphasis on women, Gentiles, and the poor, but also in his emphasis on the mercy of God. Finally, Luke is a master storyteller who gifts us with a number of wonderful stories and parables not found in the other Gospels.

With all these things in mind, I pray that those who use this book will find it to be a helpful guide for their own spiritual journey. Pastors, always on the lookout for new preaching resources, may well find help in the Commentary and Reflection sections of the meditations. But praying scripture offers more than a quick insight into a difficult text. The Gospel should be read and prayed from beginning to end over an extended period of time. Only in this way can we begin to appreciate the subtle meanings and connections that Luke had in mind when he wrote his "orderly account."

I want to acknowledge several persons who have been my companions in this, my most recent journey through the Gospel According to Luke. One is my wife, Edie, who has afforded me countless hours of solitude needed to read, pray, study, and write. She has also been an excellent critic and proofreader, adding a generous (and badly needed) sprinkling of commas to my otherwise overlong sentences! I am grateful also to members of the church I serve who have encouraged me to write and have listened patiently to my new insights. Among these are Vivian Fahey and Bridget Deprey who, for several years, have been faithful participants with me in a weekly study of the lectionary. Kathrine Laycock has been helpful in several ways, not the least of which was her writing the haiku found at the end of the chapter, "Using the Meditations in Groups."

There are others (most of whom I have never even met) who have also been companions on this journey. They are the scholars of Luke who provide us with endless insight and inspiration about his Gospel. Among the dozen or so whose commentaries I have consulted regularly, I want to mention three that I have found particularly helpful. Fred Craddock's *Luke* (John Knox Press, 1990) is a refreshingly wonderful blend of scholarly expertise and pastoral insight. Joseph Fitzmyer's two-volume *The Gospel According to Luke,* in the Anchor Bible Series (Doubleday, 1981, 1985) is awesome in its scope and depth, yet still manages to be "user friendly." Finally, Eugene LaVerdiere's *Luke* (Liturgical Press, 1990) offers a literary as well as a scholarly understanding of Luke, without forgetting the relationship of the Gospel to the early church.

A brief comment about "kingdom" language is in order. Luke uses the term *kingdom of God* more often than the other three Gospels combined. In the New Revised Standard Version Mark uses it fourteen times; Matthew, five times; and John only twice. Matthew prefers the term *kingdom of heaven,* which is not found in any of the other Gospels. In common usage the word *kingdom* usually suggests a political, if not a geographical, reality. The kingdom theology of the Gospels, however, points us more in the direction of a spiritual reality. Consider, for example, Jesus' teaching in Luke 17:21 that "the kingdom of God is among you" (NRSV). For this reason and the fact that the word *kingdom* has strong masculine connotations, a number of scholars have begun to use "the reign of God" instead. The New American Bible also does so frequently, translating Jesus' teaching to read, "the reign of God is already in your midst." As those who use this book will notice, I have also chosen to move in the direction of using *reign* in place of *kingdom*.

Finally, I want to share my belief that those who would take the gospel seriously must begin by recognizing that, from beginning to end, it is *counter-cultural*. In the reign of God the values of the world are turned upside-down. Furthermore, the reign of God is not a theology of "pie in the sky" sometime in the future. As various translations of Luke 17:21 point out, it is already "within us," "among us," "in our midst," or "all around us." We are invited to open our eyes and ears, repent of our sins, and participate in God's reign here and now. Therefore, with thanksgiving to Luke for his "orderly account" and prophetic spirit, let us join with Mary in singing praise to God:

> *The arm of the Lord is strong,*
> > *and has scattered the proud in their conceit.*
> *God has brought down the powerful from their thrones, and*
> > *lifted up the lowly;*
> *God has filled the hungry with good things,*
> > *and sent the rich away empty.*
> *God has helped his servant Israel,*
> > *remembering to have mercy,*
> > *according to the promise made to our ancestors,*
> > *to Abraham and his descendants forever.*
> > (Luke 1:51-55, AP)

Milwaukee
Pentecost 1992

PRAYING SCRIPTURE

One day Jesus was praying in a certain place. When he had finished, one
of his disciples said to him, "Lord, teach us to pray. . . ."
(Luke 11:1, TEV)

ASK ANYONE WHAT BOOKS ARE FOR and the answer will likely be,
"books are for reading." We read different kinds of books for
different reasons. We read novels for pleasure or escape. We read
textbooks to learn. We read various kinds of manuals for
technical information. We read religious books for inspiration.
And so on and on with dictionaries, artbooks, do-it-yourself
books, children's books, books of poetry, travel guides,
biographies, etc.

But what about the Bible?

Years ago I found in my grandmother's Bible a newspaper
clipping that compares the Bible to a library. The clipping directs
the reader to various "rooms" in the Bible where one can find:
history, poetry, prophecy, law, inspiration, letters, Gospels, etc. In
another old family Bible I found a comprehensive index to such
topics as: adversity, courage, creation, faith, fear, heaven, hope,
marriage, money, prayer, temptation, etc. Still another Bible
contained a bookmark offering "six good reasons why you
should join worldwide Bible reading." Bible reading, the
bookmark proclaims, "has been found highly effective by millions
of people of all ages." "Reading the Bible . . . helps you develop a
happy and useful life," was another reason. Yet another was, "the
more faithfully you read God's Word, the more you will learn to
treasure it and the greater will be the influence of its transforming
teachings on your life."[1]

It is both interesting and revealing that most of these
popular approaches to the Bible begin with the assumption that
the Bible is first of all a book and, therefore, something to be read.

This, no doubt, reflects the tendency of western culture to approach religion as it does many other things, with the head rather than the heart. While *feelings* are a primary component of our spirituality, we are more likely to define it as something we *think* about.

This book, like my *Like Trees That Grow Beside a Stream: Praying through the Psalms*, published in 1991, is based on the assumption that while reading, study, and reflection are important and even essential ways of using the Bible, it is also a book that we ought to pray. In Orthodox theology there is an understanding that icons are not just paintings representing persons and events from our spiritual history; an icon represents the spiritual presence of the person. Therefore, to be in the presence of an icon is almost like being in the presence of that person, be it Jesus or one of the saints of the church. I like to think of the scriptures in much the same way. They are more than ordinary writings. When we pray as well as study the scriptures, we can, in some mysterious sense, stand in the spiritual presence of our biblical ancestors. We are there beside Abraham as God takes him outside his tent to look up at the star-filled sky; we experience the sustaining presence of the Lord with our ancestors on the long Exodus journey; we are there with Mary as she ponders the birth of the one God has promised; and we sit at table in the home of Simon the Pharisee as an unnamed woman washes Jesus' feet with her tears and dries them with her hair.

PRAYING WITH THE HEART

To pray scripture means to enter into relationship with its truth, not just by thinking about it, but by experiencing it with our whole being. Theophan the Recluse, a monk of nineteenth-century Russia, said, "one must descend with the mind into the heart, and there stand before the face of the Lord, ever-present, all-seeing, within you."[2] The word *heart* here should not be understood in the western sense, which sees the heart as the seat of sentiment or emotion. Rather it is used in the Hebrew sense, referring to our wholeness, including our physical, intellectual, emotional, and moral attributes. In *The Way of the Heart*, Henri

Nouwen comments, "Prayer is standing in the presence of God with the mind in the heart; that is, at that point of our being where there are no divisions or distinctions and where we are totally one. There God's Spirit dwells and there the great encounter takes place."[3]

The idea of praying with the heart is not new. It is rooted in the desert spirituality practiced by hundreds of devout women and men who fled from urban life to seek God in the deserts of Palestine, Egypt, and Arabia during the fourth century. These desert fathers and mothers thrived on their austere spiritual disciplines and profoundly influenced the course of Christian history. The writings of the desert fathers and mothers are available today in several editions, including Thomas Merton's *Wisdom of the Desert Fathers*. In his insightful introduction Merton notes that "Prayer was the very heart of the desert life, and consisted of psalmody (vocal prayer—recitation of the Psalms and other parts of the Scriptures which everyone had to know by heart) and contemplation."[4]

But praying the scriptures may well be even older than these saints of the desert. It could be argued that Jesus himself not only knew, studied, and quoted scripture, but prayed it as well. If his sermons, teachings, and everyday conversation were filled with quotations and allusions to scripture, it seems likely that scripture also played an important part in his private prayer. Luke, as we shall see, often mentions that Jesus went off "to a lonely place to pray." But the most direct persuasive evidence is to be found in his prayers from the cross. His "Father, forgive them; for they do not know what they are doing," reflects Psalm 22; and his final words, "Father, into your hands I commend my spirit," came from Psalm 31.

In our time this "prayer of the heart" is sometimes described as a combination of centering prayer and discursive meditation on a passage of scripture. Its roots are in the 1500-year-old practice of prayer known in the monastic tradition by its Latin name, *lectio divina*, or divine reading. Thomas Keating provides a helpful summary of *lectio* in his book, *The Heart of the World:*

Each period of *lectio divina* follows the same plan: reflection on the Word of God, followed by free expression of the spontaneous feelings that arise in our hearts. The whole gamut of human response to truth, beauty, goodness, and love, is possible. As the heart reaches out in longing for God, it begins to penetrate the words of the sacred text. Mind and heart are united and rest in the presence of Christ. *Lectio divina* is a way of meditation that leads naturally to spontaneous prayer, and little by little, to moments of contemplation—to insights into the Word of God and the deeper meaning and significance of the truths of faith.[5]

Some who read this book will already be familiar with centering prayer or praying scripture, in which case a quick review of this chapter may be sufficient. Hopefully, those who have not yet experienced this method of Christian prayer will find it both informative and useful.

CENTERING PRAYER

Before continuing further it will be helpful to distinguish between "centering" and "praying scripture." Simply put, praying scripture is the use of a brief passage of scripture as the basis for a period of prayer or meditation. Centering prayer clears the mind of extraneous thoughts and the body of stress as a means of preparing one's self to pray scripture. The term *centering prayer* has come into common usage in recent years, largely through the writing and teaching of Father Basil Pennington, a Trappist monk of St. Joseph's Abbey in Spencer, Massachusetts.

Centering prayer is a way of our getting in touch with what the Quaker mystic, Thomas Kelly, has called the "Divine Center" within us.[6] As such, it is a way of enhancing one's experience of prayer even apart from the use of scripture. Centering prayer, or more simply, centering, seems to be a universal practice. While it has been a part of Christian spirituality for many centuries, it is also practiced by Buddhists, Jews, and Moslems, as well as by many who profess no religion.

Lawrence LeShan in *How to Meditate* describes well the need for centering when he says that "if our bodies were half as unresponsive to our will as our minds are, we would never get across the street alive."[7] A simple illustration will convince almost anyone of the truth of LeShan's statement. Try to sit for five minutes in a quiet room without thinking about anything. Or try to sit for five minutes and think of only one thing. How busy our brains are! We are always engaged in the process of taking in new information, reflecting on it, worrying about it, and filing it away in our memories. In five minutes or less we may think about a dozen or more related and unrelated things. In fact we may well find ourselves thinking of just about anything except the one thing we are trying to think about. When a cook's thoughts are often interrupted, the result may be something less than a culinary delight! When a student takes an examination in mathematics with a wandering mind, the grade may well be less than desired. No wonder our experiences of prayer often seem to be sidetracked by other thoughts.

Simply put, centering is a practice by which we attempt to discipline our minds to think for a time about one thing rather than many things. This is done by concentrating on a single thing, while gently letting go of all other thoughts. The one thing may be an object, such as a candle or an icon. Or it may be a word or a biblical phrase. It can be anything you are comfortable with, such as the constant sound of a ticking clock or a dripping faucet. Focusing on one thing is not prayer. Rather it is a means of getting one's mind, body, and spirit ready to pray.

THE METHOD OF CENTERING

One popular method of centering is to sit quietly and try to think of nothing except counting your breaths as you exhale. Simply count "one" as you breath out the first breath, "two" the second time, etc. When you come to the fourth breath, return to one rather than counting to higher numbers, which may become a distraction in itself. "One . . . two . . . three . . . four; one . . . two . . . three . . . four; one . . . two . . . three . . . four" becomes a pattern. Count only up to four, and then begin over again.

After a very short time, you will undoubtedly have the experience of being distracted by other thoughts, or you will find yourself counting beyond four! Don't worry. It's perfectly normal, and even those who have been centering for a long time have the same problem. When you become aware of the distraction, just let it go very gently. Say to yourself, "That is not why I'm here just now; I can come back to it later." Then return to your breath counting. This will happen repeatedly. Accept it and continue the discipline of counting your breaths.

It may be several weeks before you begin to achieve some measure of discipline over your wandering mind. Don't let it worry you. It is simply part of being human. The thoughts that interrupt your attempts to become centered may be things you are worried about, things you need to accomplish during the day, or thoughts about something you did recently. If you are hungry, the interrupting thoughts may be of food.

If you find it difficult to dismiss such extraneous thoughts, it may be helpful to imagine that you are sitting beside a gently burning campfire. As the interrupting thoughts come to mind, simply let them rise up and out of your vision with the smoke rising from the fire. Or if you like water, imagine yourself sitting on the sand on the bottom of a lake. The water is warm and comforting and you are surrounded by the gentle motion of plants in the water. Allow your interrupting thoughts to float up and disappear from your vision like bubbles of air rising to the surface.

Posture can be an important part of centering, especially if you have back problems. Sit erect in a comfortable, but fairly straight chair with both feet resting firmly on the floor. Let your hands relax in your lap. Hold your head in a balanced position so that it will not bob forward or sideways as you relax. Imagine your head being supported by a string attached to the ceiling.

Consciously relax the muscles in various parts of your body, beginning with your feet and moving upward to the legs, hips, back, neck, arms, and finally the muscles in your face. Sense where the tension is in each set of muscles, and let it go. Most of us tend to carry tension in our faces with tightened muscles in the forehead and around the mouth. Let them all relax. After your body is relaxed, take three or four slow, *deep* breaths to help remove any remaining tension. Hold the breath for a few seconds, and then let it out slowly, breathing out the tension. Then, with your body relaxed, begin counting your breaths up to four, over and over, letting go of all extraneous thoughts. Continue for fifteen minutes or more until you feel centered.

The meditations in this book each begin with a suggested preparation which will help you to get ready to pray the particular passage of scripture. Those in the earlier meditations are especially directed toward the process of centering itself. The preparations suggested in later meditations will often relate more directly to the content of the scripture. Remember that centering is very worthwhile by itself. It is a wonderful means of relaxation. It is a good way to release tension in your body as well as in your mind. Once you have become comfortable with it, you may find it helpful to do even one or two minutes of centering as you take a break from your work during the day. Centering is prayerful in itself because it helps us to get in touch with our Divine Center, where we can experience the presence of God in the relative absence of stress, tension, and distractions of the moment. One final word. If you have already learned how to center, and you feel comfortable with the method or methods you use, it is probably best to continue in your own accustomed way.

Praying Scripture

Centering is a way of preparing ourselves for the experience of praying the scriptures. Once you feel yourself to be centered, open your eyes and read the brief passage of scripture you have selected in advance. Read it *slowly* and reflectively. Then be silent for a moment, taking time to find your center again if necessary. Read the passage again, taking time to linger over any phrase or thought to which you feel attracted.

Most people find themselves particularly drawn to or teased by some phrase or verse by the time they have completed the second reading. It is not necessary to say to yourself, "I need to look for a thought I like." If you are centered and open, the thought or phrase will likely find you rather than your looking for it. It may strike you because it speaks to a need in you at the present time. Or it may be a beautiful metaphor or a new way of understanding an old idea. It may simply be a phrase or idea that intrigues you or feels comforting or challenging. Whatever it is, come back to it after you have finished your second reading.

Repeat that phrase or thought a few times. Let your mind play with it. Reflect on it. Ask yourself, "Why this particular thought? What might it be saying to me? What words seem to stand out in it? How might this insight be incorporated into my own life? How does it relate to things that are happening to me right now?"

In the meditations offered in this book, a phrase or thought has already been chosen from the Gospel reading. This has been done intentionally to help those who are praying the scriptures for the first time develop a sense of how the experience flows from centering, to reading the passage, to reflecting on the theme or phrase, and finally to the incorporation of that idea in your own informal prayer. You may want to pray all the readings as they are offered in the book. Or you may decide to read the passage from your Bible and trust the process to produce a phrase or thought that addresses you. In either case, take time to reflect on the thought, play with it, ask questions related to it, and otherwise search out its relationship to who and where you are at this point in your life.

After you have reflected on the phrase or thought for a few moments, you will likely come to a point when you have a sense of having completed that part of your prayer. That is the time to move on to offer your own prayer to God in whatever style feels comfortable to you. You may want to share with God any insights and learnings you have had from your reading and reflection. You may want to ask God to help you to understand something in your meditation that feels unfinished. Or you may want to ask for help with a particular situation in your life. Perhaps you simply need to ask for greater understanding or clarity about something.

Take time for your prayer. Allow yourself to listen to what God might be saying to you as well as what you are saying to God. If what you are praying over seems to call for an action or response on your part, try to choose some *achievable* goal related to the prayer experience and ask God to help you to accomplish that goal in your life. When your prayer is finished, you may find it helpful to end with a favorite blessing, the Lord's Prayer, or some other act which is meaningful to you. Let this become part of your ongoing ritual each time you pray.

KEEPING A PRAYER JOURNAL

One last suggestion. You may find that the discipline of praying scripture is enhanced if you take just a moment after each prayer experience to record four simple things in a prayer notebook or journal. This need not be long or complicated. Simply note:
1) the date;
2) the scripture passage used (e.g. Luke 12:32-34);
3) the particular phrase or verse which struck you (e.g. "Your heart will always be where your riches are.");
4) a brief, personal note about any insight or feeling which resulted from this prayer experience.

Such a record is not time consuming and will become more and more valuable after several months or years of praying scripture. In years to come, it will very likely become an important source of valuable information about your own spiritual growth—information that may otherwise be lost in the process.

AN INVITATION TO LUKE'S GOSPEL

Dear Theophilus:
Many people have done their best to write a report of the things that
have taken place among us. They wrote what we have been told by those
who saw these things from the beginning and who proclaimed the
message. And so, Your Excellency, because I have carefully studied all
these matters from their beginning, I thought it would be good to write
an orderly account for you.
(Luke 1:1-3, TEV)

LUKE-ACTS

AFTER MANY YEARS of excellent biblical scholarship, numerous questions remain about the identity of the author of the Gospel According to Luke, his background, sources, and reasons for writing. While it is possible that some of these questions could be answered with the discovery of new information in the future, it seems unlikely. One thing is certain, however. The Gospel According to Luke and the Book of Acts are two volumes of one work produced by a single author. Even though they are not found together in ancient manuscripts and are separated by the Gospel of John in our modern Bibles, virtually all scholars view Luke's two volumes as a single literary effort and refer to it as Luke-Acts.

Both volumes open with a prologue addressed to "Theophilus," who is clearly a Christian and, as some have suggested, may have been Luke's patron. The prologue to the Gospel provides Luke's stated purpose for writing. The prologue to Acts is both a short summary of the first volume and a connecting link to the second. The author, with an obvious interest in history, sees his first volume as "the time of Jesus," which ended with the resurrection, and his second volume as "the time of the church," which began with the Pentecost event.[8]

Together, Luke-Acts constitutes more than one-fourth of the New Testament. Not even the combined length of Paul's letters can match the volume of Luke's contribution.

WHO WAS LUKE?

According to Christian tradition, the author of Luke-Acts was none other than the co-worker and traveling companion of Paul, mentioned in Colossians 4:14 as "Luke, the beloved physician." Luke is also mentioned by Paul in Philemon 24, "Epaphras, who is in prison with me for the sake of Christ Jesus, sends you his greetings, and so do my fellow workers Mark, Aristarchus, Demas, and Luke." Luke is named a third time in the Second Letter to Timothy (4:11). Modern scholarship, however, has cast serious doubt on the previously assumed Pauline authorship of both First and Second Timothy.

Some have seen additional evidence for Luke's relationship with Paul in several "we" passages in the Book of Acts that seem to indicate that the author was with Paul on at least several occasions (Acts 16:10-17; 20:5-15; 21:1-18; and 27:1–28:16). But, again, recent scholars have suggested other explanations for these passages and point out inconsistencies between the "we" passages and other information in Paul's letters. Various other arguments have been raised both for and against the possibility that the author of Luke-Acts was a companion of Paul. The fact remains that we simply do not have enough information to provide a definitive answer to the question of Luke's relationship with Paul.

While it is not possible to know everything we would like to know about Luke, there is still much that we do know. It is clear that he was well educated and cosmopolitan in his outlook. He wrote in excellent Greek. He was a competent historian of broad learning and deep faith. His home was not in Palestine, but in Asia Minor, possibly in or near Antioch, the political and cultural capital of the Roman province of Syria. One scholar, Joseph Fitzmyer, ventures to be even more specific, saying, "I regard Luke as a Gentile Christian, not, however, as a Greek, but as a non-Jewish Semite, a native of Antioch, where he was well educated in a Hellenistic atmosphere and culture."[9]

Among the many interesting "traditions" about Luke is one that calls him the first Christian artist or, more specifically, the first painter of icons. Some of the best known virgin and child icons, such as the "Virgin of Vladimir" and the "Odegitria Virgin" are often said to have been painted from Lucan prototypes. The original of the Odegitria Virgin is said by Weitzmann, Chatzidakis, and Radojcic in their book *Icons* (Alpine Fine Arts Collection, Ltd., New York: 1980), to have been painted by Luke and brought to Constantinople from Jerusalem in the fifth century. Unfortunately, there is no evidence to support this tradition, and most scholars have suggested that the stories of Luke the icon painter probably originated in the Middle Ages.

WHEN AND FOR WHOM DID LUKE WRITE?

The destruction of Jerusalem and the Temple by the Romans in the year 70 C.E. brought about a new religious and political situation affecting the lives, not only of Jews, but also of Gentile and Jewish Christians. These new circumstances called for a retelling of the Christian story. It is likely that the Gospels of Matthew and Luke were both written to address this need. It has long been assumed that Matthew was intended primarily for the Jewish Christian community and that Luke was written with Gentile Christians in mind.

Most of Luke's readers lived in the territory surrounding Antioch, which was one of the great centers of Christian missionary activity. They, and perhaps Luke himself, were products of missionary efforts under the auspices of Paul. Because of this history they saw missionary activity as a normal way of spreading the gospel. The same area around Antioch was also home for Matthew's community. But for the latter it was, as Eugene LaVerdiere says, "a home away from home, a home in the diaspora in which they were now called to sink permanent roots."[10]

Thus both Luke and Matthew wrote at least in part to reinterpret the earlier Gospel of Mark for a new generation of

Christians who found themselves fifty years removed from Jesus' death, geographically removed from Jerusalem (now destroyed), and struggling to live the demands of the gospel in a Gentile world.

Luke undoubtedly had other reasons for his writing. One recent scholar, Luke Timothy Johnson, says, "Luke's purposes are not determined by a momentary crisis or by doctrinal deviance, but by the very existence of a messianic sect in the Gentile world."[11] Johnson suggests that, among other purposes, Luke-Acts was intended as an apology for the Christian movement in a Gentile world, arguing that, "The Christians were politically harmless and should be allowed the same freedom given by Rome to 'other Jews.'"[12]

While it was certainly not one of Luke's major purposes in writing, it is worth mentioning that he seems to have had a special interest in explaining why the world had not yet ended as predicted in Mark 13:30, a passage Luke also included in his own Gospel. This question has continued to be of concern to a relatively small number of "eschatological Christians" up to and including our own time. According to William Baird, Luke's answer comes in a theology that divides history into three eras, "the time of the Jews, which is finished; the time of Jesus Christ, which is the key to history; and the time of the church, which is now." The time of the church may thus be "extended into the distant future so that the time of the end remains remote."[13]

The date of Luke's writing, like his identity, is difficult to establish. As he acknowledges in his prologue, he was not an eyewitness to the gospel events. Since he seems to have knowledge of the destruction of Jerusalem, he must have written after 70 C.E. The question then, is, how much later could he have written? While various arguments serve to narrow down the dates, none is absolutely convincing. Some have suggested that the experience of the church implied by Luke-Acts fits well within the political situation during the reign of the Emperor Domitian, which covered the period from 81–96 C.E. Most scholars are in agreement with this span of time, though some offer a narrower range of dates, usually between 80 and 90.

WHAT WERE LUKE'S SOURCES?

While more specific references will be made in the introductions to individual meditations later in the book, a general comment is in order here concerning Luke's sources. In the prologue of his Gospel Luke recognizes the witness and work of those who have already "done their best to write a report on the things that have taken place among us" (1:1, TEV). As such he is not trying to replace Mark's Gospel, but rather to offer a fuller account for a new generation of Christians who live in different circumstances. Indeed he used Mark as his primary source, including more than half of it in his own Gospel. This is not to say that he always used the Markan material exactly as he found it. He frequently recast it in his own style and for his own purposes, often improving on the quality of Mark's Greek. He also eliminated some of the terms, such as *Golgotha, Gethsemane,* and *rabbi* that would have been foreign to his intended readers.

He did, however, retain the basic outline of Mark, into which he inserted material from at least two additional sources. The first is called by scholars, *Q,* for the German *Quelle,* meaning "source." About 250 of the approximately 1100 verses in Luke come from *Q* and are also found in Matthew's Gospel. There is also a sizable amount of additional material, found only in Luke, and therefore called by some scholars the *L* source. Very little is known about the *Q* and *L* sources, and they continue to be important topics of discussion and debate among biblical scholars.

SOME CHARACTERISTICS OF LUKE'S GOSPEL

Every writer has a unique style which to a greater or lesser degree tells us something about his or her personality. For example, it would be very difficult for anyone to read many of Paul's letters without drawing some conclusions about his personality (words like *impulsive, bold, paternalistic, strong-willed,* and *proud* come to mind). Others write in a style offering far fewer opportunities for us to draw many conclusions about their personality. Luke is such a writer.

Even so, a careful examination of Luke-Acts will provide the sensitive reader with at least some impressionistic clues about the kind of person he was. Jerome Kodell, in the introduction to his brief commentary on Luke, says, "Dante called Luke the 'scribe of Christ's gentleness' because of his emphasis on Jesus' mercy to sinners and outcasts. Some of the most memorable gospel stories of divine mercy are found only in Luke ("the widow of Nain, the prodigal son, Zacchaeus").[14] While it is only a matter of speculation, it may be that this emphasis is the result of Luke's own gentle spirit.

Luke was a gifted storyteller. His narrative "communicates by presenting the story in such a way that the readers enter the story and discover that it is their own."[15] The comments of the narrator are so skillfully woven into the story that the reader often does not notice being provided with information unknown to the characters themselves. The order in which Luke presents his material is also masterful. While it may sometimes appear chaotic to the casual reader, the themes subtly play off one another, drawing our attention to otherwise unnoticed connections and reminding us of related themes from other parts of the Gospel. Sometimes Luke juxtaposes seemingly unrelated material for no apparent reason, when in reality he may have had a purpose in mind. It is possible, for example, that the parable of the Good Samaritan and the story of Jesus' visit to the home of Mary and Martha (both unique to Luke) are placed next to one another to point out that, while action may be the proper response in one situation, other occasions may call not for action, but reflection.

Another characteristic of the Gospel is Luke's interest in prayer and his depiction of Jesus as a person of prayer. He clearly went out of his way to add an element of prayer to passages whose parallels in the other Gospels make no mention of it. Neither Matthew nor Mark, for example, mentions prayer in connection with the baptism of Jesus. Yet Luke, whose baptism account is even shorter than Mark's, goes out of his way to add, "While he was praying, heaven was opened . . ."(3:21, TEV).

Mark's account of the calling of the twelve disciples (3:13-19) makes no mention of prayer, nor does Matthew. Yet Luke has Jesus spend a whole night in prayer before choosing his disciples (6:12). Similar added references to prayer are to be found in Luke's accounts of Peter's declaration (9:18-21), the Transfiguration (9:28), Jesus' prediction of Peter's denial (22:32), and Jesus' teaching the disciples how to pray (11:1). It is obvious that Luke had a special interest in prayer.

LUKE'S KNOWLEDGE OF THE HEBREW SCRIPTURES

As many have noted, Luke's knowledge and use of the Hebrew Scriptures in the writing of his Gospel was extensive, especially considering his Gentile background. Fred Craddock says:

> The fact is that Luke makes more use of the Old Testament than will be observed by a casual reader or by someone not familiar with those texts. The reason is that Luke often uses Scripture in an indirect or allusive way, apparently assuming that the readers will catch the connections. But what is more impressive is that Luke will often tell a story about Jesus or one of the early church leaders after the manner, and sometimes in the very words, of an Old Testament story. For example, Mary's song is Hannah's song (1 Sam. 2:1-10); the boy Jesus in the temple is the boy Samuel in the temple at Shiloh (1 Sam. 2–3; note especially 2:26); and Jesus raises a widow's son in an account most similar to that of Elijah's raising a widow's son (1 Kings 17:17-24).[16]

Craddock goes on to wonder about the popular assumption that "Matthew is the Jewish Gospel, Luke is the Gentile Gospel." If Luke is a Gentile, he asks, how is it that he is so knowledgeable of the Hebrew Scriptures and respectful of their authority? And why does he assume that his readers also know and respect the Hebrew Scriptures? Why does he "insist on more continuity between temple and church, between synagogue and church, than any other New Testament writer?"[17] Such questions, particularly intriguing in light of Luke's assumed Gentile background and audience, must be left to the scholars.

LUKE'S PROPHETIC SPIRIT

Luke's knowledge of the Hebrew Scriptures is nowhere more evident than in his use of prophetic themes. LaVerdiere calls prophetic writing "Luke's most basic theological inspiration" and goes on to point to Luke's introduction of John the Baptist in 3:1-2 as fundamental in the establishment of Luke-Acts as a prophetic history.[18] But even prior to this classic prophetic introduction are the deeply prophetic themes sounded by "Mary's Song" and "Zechariah's Prophecy" in the opening chapter.

Both Matthew and Mark recognize Jesus' prophetic ministry when they tell the story of his teaching in the synagogue in Nazareth. But their accounts pale in comparison with Luke, who has Jesus reading from the sixty-first chapter of Isaiah and then boldly proclaiming that his own ministry marks the fulfillment of Isaiah's prophetic vision. Prophetic themes are a hallmark of Luke, who sees Jesus bringing salvation to those who need it most: sinners, tax collectors, Samaritans, Gentiles, and the poor. Twice in chapter 14, Luke calls for the inclusion of "the poor, the crippled, the lame, and the blind" in the reign of God.

THE ROLE OF WOMEN IN LUKE

Luke, unlike the other evangelists, seems to have gone out of his way to include additional references to women in his Gospel and to lift up the role played by women in the ministry of Jesus. Indeed, there are more references to women in Luke than in Matthew and Mark combined. It is also striking that so many of these are found in the so-called L source, including the stories of Elizabeth and Mary in the birth narratives; the prophetess Anna in the presentation story; the raising of the widow's son at Nain; Jesus' visit to Mary and Martha; the parable of the lost coin; the parable of the widow and the judge; and the naming of several among the "many other women who used their own resources to help Jesus and his disciples" (8:1-3).

Luke's portrayal of women must be viewed in the light of his concern to present the gospel favorably against the prevailing norms of Jewish and Roman culture. Whether or not these additional references constitute a special Lucan sensitivity to the needs and contributions of women is a question worthy of continuing study. Some may see them as further evidence of Luke's prophetic spirit and of his desire to recognize an expanded role for women in the church.

While Luke can hardly be called a feminist, even when measured against the cultural attitudes of his own time, I must disagree with the negative way his Gospel has been portrayed by one scholar in particular. In *The Women's Bible Commentary*, published in 1992, Jane Schaberg refers to the third Gospel as "an extremely dangerous text, perhaps the most dangerous in the Bible."[19] Luke, she says, "deftly portrays [women] as models of subordinate service, excluded from the power center of the movement and from significant responsibilities."[20] She further accuses him of "incorporating and editing material, subtly making the point that women must be restricted."[21] "Luke's intent," she says, "is to undermine the leadership of women."[22] In her summary statement, Schaberg concludes that "enthusiasm for Luke-Acts, the most massive work in the New Testament, is enthusiasm for a formidable opponent, not for an ally."[23]

In her zeal to condemn, Schaberg makes a number of statements that seem contradictory. She says, for example, that "One of the strategies of this Gospel is to provide female readers with female characters as role models: prayerful, quiet, grateful women, supportive of male leadership, forgoing the prophetic ministry."[24] Yet a few pages later she refers to the Magnificat as "the great New Testament song of liberation—personal and social, moral and economic—a revolutionary document of intense conflict and victory," and goes on to speak of Mary as both evangelist and prophet![25] In another place she states that "No women in Luke, by word or action, identify Jesus as Messiah or Son of God."[26] What then are we to make of Mary's response to the annunciation, halting and questioning though it is, or of the witness she makes in the Magnificat? And what about Anna, whose response in the presentation story implies, not only a recognition of the Messiah, but a fervent witness "to all who were looking for the redemption of Jerusalem"?

Schaberg states that Luke's Gospel "has no scene that illustrates release for an abused woman, freeing her from low self-esteem, guilt, and masochism as well as from the brutality and intimidation of another. . . ."[27] To this we must ask, was not the woman who washed Jesus' feet with her tears the victim of verbal abuse and intimidation by the Pharisees? And was she not released from her guilt and low self-esteem by Jesus' forgiveness? And what about the parable of the widow and the judge? Was the widow not abused by the denial of her rights and was she not released from that abuse after persisting in her quest for justice? Such a woman can hardly be described as quiet and submissive! Luke's stated objective in the parable is to illustrate persistence in prayer, but it is hard to imagine him choosing such an example if his own view was that "women must be restricted"! Finally, after admitting that women do speak prophetically in Luke, Schaberg complains that "they suffer as prophets no one hears."[28] Here we must ask, how does their not being heard make these female prophets different from their male counterparts?

There can be no doubt that the Bible was written in the context of a patriarchal culture and that sexist assumptions thus abound throughout biblical literature. Nor can there be any doubt that, until recently, biblical commentators (most of them male) have failed to explore these questions adequately. We are fortunate now to live in a time when feminist scholarship does examine such matters and often points the way to a more balanced interpretation of scripture. Unfortunately, Schaberg's strident statements generate more heat than light for those who seek a better understanding of the role of women in Luke's Gospel. A more objective and helpful treatment of Luke's view of women may be found in Gail R. O'Day's article on Acts, also found in *The Women's Bible Commentary*.

USING THE MEDITATIONS

Then Jesus told his disciples a parable to teach them that they should always pray and never become discouraged.
(Luke 18:1, TEV)

As NOTED IN THE OPENING CHAPTER, praying scripture goes back at least as far as the fourth century, when it was practiced by the fathers and mothers of the desert. Since that time it has been a part of the 1500-year-old monastic practice of *lectio* and used by many others as well. In the secular world of the twentieth century, however, this form of Christian prayer has largely been forgotten. Among Protestants it has been almost unheard of since the time of the Reformation. That changed with the new spirit of openness brought about by the Second Vatican Council. Now Catholics and Protestants share in the rediscovery of many elements of our common spiritual tradition.

The meditations in this book and in *Like Trees That Grow Beside a Stream* are offered in the hope of encouraging modern Christians to recover the richness of prayer deeply rooted in scripture. The meditations offered here are intended to serve as a "user friendly" introduction to make praying scripture easier for those who might otherwise think of it as too difficult or too foreign to their own experience. It is my hope that those who decide to follow the format and suggestions that accompany the meditations will soon feel comfortable enough to pick up their Bibles and begin praying whatever parts of it they choose, including perhaps a daily or weekly lectionary.

The meditations cover the whole of the Gospel According to Luke. This has been done in part to provide those interested with easy access to explanatory and interpretive material often available only in biblical commentaries. Such commentaries are often both expensive and filled with terms and concepts not easily understood by those unfamiliar with modern biblical scholarship.

Another reason for including all of the Gospel is to demonstrate that in choosing biblical passages for prayer we should not limit ourselves to selected texts which seem to lend themselves to reflection. Those who approach the praying of scripture in faith and openness will soon discover that almost any part of scripture is worthy of prayerful consideration.

THE FORMAT OF THE MEDITATIONS

With these things in mind let us move now to a brief summary of the format used in the meditations, followed by additional suggestions for use as you discover how to pray the scriptures. The format for each meditation is as follows:

Commentary: Information is provided about Luke's sources; his reasons for including particular material; the relationship of the passage to those that precede and follow it; and other information which may be helpful in understanding and appropriating the meaning of the passage in your own situation.

Preparation: This section offers suggestions for getting ready to pray the passage in the context of "centering prayer."

Reading: At this point suggestions are made about the actual reading of the passage, usually asking that it be read at least twice.

Reflection: The reflection section offers suggested questions and observations to stimulate personal reflection and meditation on the passage.

Prayer: Following a period of reflection, a possible approach to prayer is suggested, related to the theme of the passage.

COMMENTARY

Anyone who has ever studied Shakespeare will know that reading and understanding sixteenth century English can be both rewarding and frustrating. Words that meant one thing in Shakespeare's time often mean something very different today.

We need help in order to understand words, customs, humor, and political and historical allusions that we no longer use or that may be used in different ways today. For these reasons we are well advised not to sit down and try to read a Shakespeare play without a good annotated version to guide us.

If such a guide is needed to understand Shakespeare who wrote only four hundred years ago and in our own language, think how much more we need a guide to help us understand the Bible! We are fortunate to live in a time when there are several excellent English translations of the Bible available. But the availability of modern translations is not enough. As any serious reader of the Bible knows, there is in almost any passage of scripture, "more than meets the eye." It may be a word with subtle or double meanings, or the way the original language is translated into English. It may be a social or religious custom of biblical times, a measurement or some other technical term unfamiliar to us. It may have to do with the writer's reasons for locating a passage in a particular context in order to call attention to things that have gone before or will come afterward. These are only a few of the many things that can get in the way of our understanding the meaning of scripture. It is as important to give our attention to these details as it is to take time to look up unfamiliar words when we engage in other kinds of reading.

That is why biblical scholars have labored to produce sophisticated commentaries on every book of the Bible, asking and answering questions most of us would never dream of. While the Gospel According to Luke fills only forty to fifty pages in most Bibles, commentaries on it are often many times that long. One of the best currently available commentaries on Luke consists of two heavy volumes totalling more than 1600 pages. While this may sound like a "head trip" rather than the "heart trip" I encouraged in an earlier chapter, it is the kind of homework we need to do in order to more fully understand the meaning of the scripture we wish to pray.

Therefore, in order to ease the burden on those who may be new to praying scripture, I have provided a brief introductory commentary for each of the gospel meditations. A thoughtful reading of this introduction will provide answers to many of the questions you are likely to encounter in your reading and praying of that passage. Should you wish to explore the background of the text in greater depth you may want to consult any of the many fine commentaries available, some of which may be found in the selected bibliography.

Preparation

The suggestions for preparation have been designed to be helpful for those who have had little or no experience with centering prayer. In the earlier meditations these suggestions offer ways of learning how to become centered, in order to be more relaxed and focused in the actual experience of praying the biblical passage. My suggestions follow one approach to centering and may vary in some details from those of others. If you have already had experience with centering and feel comfortable with your own method, you should by all means feel free to continue according to your own practice. For those with little or no experience, the following checklist may be helpful. Don't feel that you have to "get it all right" the first time. You won't! Remember how busy and fragmented our lives often are. It will take a while, even to give yourself permission to be quiet and peaceful, much less to achieve it.

1) Before you begin your centering be sure you have your Bible handy with the pre-selected scripture passage marked.

2) Begin your preparation with a moment or two of gentle exercise.

3) Sit with your back straight, feet on the floor, and your head balanced.

4) Systematically relax all the muscles in your body, taking care not to forget those in your face and neck.

5) Take three or four long, slow, deep breaths, breathing in peace and breathing out any remaining tension.

6) When you are ready, gently begin to count your breaths as you exhale. Count only up to four, then go back to one and begin again.

7) As you count, allow extraneous thoughts to drift away. Don't be discouraged when they return, as they surely will.

8) Continue counting until you feel like you have reached a state of interior peace and are ready to read and pray the pre-selected scripture passage.

READING THE PASSAGE

Don't underestimate the importance of reading your chosen scripture passage *slowly* and *reflectively*. Much of our reading is done at a fairly rapid pace, whether silently or aloud. It is therefore important to remember that scripture is not scientific or factual data to be rushed through in order to gain a general impression of its content. Nor should it be approached with the thought of getting to the point at the end. When we read and pray scripture, God may be asking us to wrestle with an idea at any point in the passage. Thus every phrase is important, every word a potential source of new challenge and insight. Take plenty of time to read the passage slowly, savoring images, reflecting on new ideas, and lingering over whatever intrigues you. After you have read it once, avoid immediately rushing back to start your second reading. Take a moment or two to relax and continue in your centering. Then, when your spirit is again quiet, go back and begin the second reading, even more slowly than before, giving attention to any phrase which seems to address you, tease you, or intrigue you.

REFLECTION AND MEDITATION

After you have finished your second reading, relax again and continue in your centering. As you do so, allow your mind to play with any ideas, words, and phrases that may have emerged during your reading. Let those words, phrases, and thoughts suggest themselves to you naturally. As they come to you, gently ask yourself, why this particular phrase or that particular word? What might it be saying to *me*? Why did I react to it the way I did? How does this theme relate to my own experience? How does it relate to what is going on in my life right now? Take plenty of time and allow the process to be spontaneous; don't rush it. Don't move on to the reflection questions and suggestions until you feel you have listened to what is happening inside you.

When you feel you are ready to move on, begin looking at the Reflection section. Read it slowly, taking time to pause and reflect on any questions or suggestions that seem appropriate. Continue with your reading and reflection as long as it seems to be productive. After you have experienced the process several times and begin to feel comfortable with it, you will likely know when you are ready to end your reflection and move on to the closing prayer.

PRAYER

Remember that you have been praying all along as you centered, read, and reflected on the scripture. Now take time to give your prayer more structure according to your *personal* pattern and experience. It may take the form of a dialogue between you and God. It may be a matter of sharing with God any feelings or questions that flow out of your reflection on the text. Or it may simply be a matter of remaining in the peace-filled silence, listening to or enjoying the presence of God. If your reflection has moved you to do something or change something in your life, be sure that the goal you set is simple and achievable. Ask God to support you in that effort. When your prayer is completed, it may be helpful to bring the time to a close by using a favorite line of scripture, the Lord's Prayer, or something else that you find personally meaningful. You may wish to choose something that can become a regular part of your ritual as you continue to pray scripture each day.

Finally, when you are ready to move on to the next activity of your day, do so slowly. Take a few deep breaths, giving yourself a moment or two to return to the state of consciousness which we shall reluctantly call, "normal." Give both mind and body time to readjust to the tasks, demands, and opportunities of the day. Avoid moving too quickly as you proceed to whatever is next on your agenda. Consciously give yourself permission to carry within you throughout the day the peace you have experienced in your time of prayer.

One more suggestion. Praying scripture does not need to end with the process outlined above. Certain words or phrases may have become important during your prayer. Insights have been received. You may have resolved to try to do something differently in your daily life. Allow such things to continue to be with you as you move on to other activities. When you least expect it, one of the phrases or insights of your prayer will suddenly pop into your mind again. When that happens take a moment to remember, to ask why it came back at this particular moment; what am I being reminded of? In this way the scripture, and your praying of it, continues throughout the day, reinforcing itself and helping you to grow in the spirit.

A Word About the Theme Phrases

The phrases I have selected as the titles for individual meditations on the Gospel are meant to serve as a focus or theme, which in most cases is carried through the reading, reflection, and prayer suggestions. Obviously you will find some of the suggested themes helpful and others less helpful. After you have had some experience praying scripture, you will no longer need a suggested theme. You may even find such themes to be too limiting. Your own theme will begin to emerge naturally as you read and pray any passage of scripture. It is the word or phrase that intrigues or teases you in your reading and reflection. It is a bit like an "aha" moment when something deep inside you recognizes that you are being personally addressed by the text. Don't force it by consciously looking for it. Instead, allow it to find you.

Perhaps it goes without saying that when you have prayed a passage of scripture once, you have by no means exhausted what it may have to say to you. It is not unusual to come back to the same passage several months or years later and discover that it speaks to you in a very different way because you are coming to it from a different place in your life. You may also find that reading the same passage later using a different translation will have the same result.

CHOOSING A BIBLE TRANSLATION

I am sometimes asked for advice about what translation of the Bible to use in praying scripture. We are fortunate to live in a time when there are many translations to choose from. They range all the way from the King James (Authorized) Version, first published in 1611, to the *Contemporary English Version New Testament*, produced by the American Bible Society in 1991. The Elizabethan language of the former gives it a quality that some, particularly those who grew up using it, may still prefer. It is, however, the same English used by Shakespeare and thus presents us with similar problems when it comes to understanding its meaning. In addition, modern biblical scholarship, together with the use of recently discovered biblical manuscripts, mean that the King James Version is no longer adequate in terms of accuracy and translation.

Of the many modern translations, opinions will differ as to which is best. From the point of view of biblical scholarship the New Revised Standard Version is probably the single most accurate translation available at the present time. The Revised English Bible, the New Jerusalem Bible, Today's English Version, and the New American Bible are also acceptable, and among these, the choice is largely a matter of personal preference. Even so, it is best not to limit one's reading to any single translation simply out of habit or convenience. A comparison of several translations will often provide fresh insight into a given text.

From the standpoint of modern biblical scholarship, there are several other contemporary English translations that are best not considered in the same category as those mentioned above. Among these are the New International Version and the New King James Version, both of which are well marketed, but may be lacking from the standpoint of accuracy. Some others, including the Living Bible, are not translations from ancient manuscripts, but simply contemporary paraphrases of earlier translations. These paraphrased versions are often very readable, but leave much to be desired from the point of view of biblical scholarship. Some of them may even present a particular theological bias.

The biblical references used in this book, including the phrases used as titles for the meditations, come from several different versions, but most notably the New Revised Standard Version (NRSV) and Today's English Version (TEV), respected for its rendering of the original texts into clear and contemporary English. When I have used other translations, they are clearly marked (NEB, NAB, JB, etc.). I would urge anyone who prays scripture regularly to have available several good translations in order to be able to compare the text for different words and nuances.

Using the Meditations in Groups

Now about eight days after these sayings Jesus took with him Peter and
John and James, and went up on the mountain to pray.
(Luke 9:28, NRSV)

WHILE THE MEDITATIONS IN THIS BOOK and the psalm meditations in *Like Trees that Grow Beside a Stream* were written primarily as a means of introducing individuals to the practice of praying scripture, their format and content can easily be adapted for use with small groups. Those who have experience leading groups in various kinds of guided meditations will have no difficulty using these meditations. Much will depend on the particular group of persons, their knowledge and experience of scripture and of each other; their experience in prayer; the amount of time available, etc. The following suggestions offer several different ways of adapting the praying of scripture for use by groups.

GUIDED MEDITATION

If the group you have in mind will be together only for one occasion, such as a retreat, you might decide to adapt a scripture passage with story qualities for use as the basis of a guided meditation. This will enable members of the group to imagine the story in their minds, listen to any dialogue contained in it, and respond later with the feelings they may have had as they allowed themselves to enter into it. If time permits it is helpful to offer some basic ideas about centering prayer before moving directly to the guided meditation.

There are many scripture passages that lend themselves to guided meditation because of their story quality, descriptive imagery, setting, etc. The story of Mary and Martha (Luke 10:38-42) might be a good choice because it can easily be imaged by participants. Most individuals can identify with either Mary or Martha in the story and later share their feelings about it. Using this or a similar passage with a small group can be as simple as inviting those in the group to quietly center themselves, then having someone read or tell the story in a way that invites individuals, not only to hear, but to enter into the story as observers or participants. Following a time to experience the story personally, the leader can offer simple questions to stimulate personal reflection. This can then lead to a time of personal (or shared) prayer on themes, observations, and challenges that arise out of the experience.

The passage of scripture chosen should determine the format of the guided meditation. In some instances it will be well to first lead the group in the meditation, inviting them to enter into the story through the use of description and imagination. This might be followed by asking participants to share what they saw or experienced, what insights they gained, etc. Following this, if you feel it would be helpful, introduce some of the questions and suggestions in the Reflection section of the meditations in the book. Likewise you will want to determine when or whether to use the introductory material.

Such a group experience might close with an invitation to revisit the scene of the meditation journey, followed by an opportunity to offer brief prayers either privately or shared with the group.

This kind of guided meditation can be a good introduction to the idea of using scripture as the basis for personal prayer. Other passages that lend themselves to such guided meditations include: the parable of the good Samaritan (Luke 10:25-37); various parts of the birth narratives in Luke 1 and 2; the healing of the paralyzed man in Luke 5:17-26; Jesus at the home of Simon the Pharisee (Luke 7:36-50); and the feeding of the five thousand (Luke 9:10-17).

COLLATION

Another way of praying scripture in a group is the way of collation. The word comes from the Latin *collatio*, which means "a bringing together." It describes a centuries old form of collective prayer used by Benedictine monks during the evening meal. The meal itself became known as the collatio. The prayer consisted of the reading from a passage of scripture or other religious book followed by a discussion or "conference" on its meaning.

Usually a brief text is read three times, after each of which the community is invited to respond. After the first reading individuals simply repeat a phrase or verse they found significant in the reading. After the second reading brief comments are made providing insight into the meaning of the chosen verse. Then, following the third reading, brief prayers or petitions may be offered, also related to the verse.

Those who use the collation as a means of praying scripture in a group usually discover that several different verses or phrases are lifted up by different individuals. This, along with the variety of insights and prayers, often provides for a rich group experience of the scripture passage in the context of prayer. Be sure to provide several moments of silence for reflection after each reading. The use of different voices for the three readings may also add to the richness of the prayer.

SCRIPTURE CONVERSATION

A variation of the collation is sometimes called a scripture conversation. As the name implies it is more oriented to conversation and less to prayer than collation. On the first reading members of the group are encouraged to respond objectively or in terms of impressions. The goal at this stage is to get at the basic facts of the passage, such as the scene, the actions, sounds, etc. A second reading may be followed by a series of questions in which the leader encourages others to become personally involved with the content of the scripture being considered. Questions like, "What troubled you?" or "What do you wonder about?" may be appropriate. A third or interpretive stage challenges the group to draw forth the implications of the reading in relationship to their personal life experiences. Ideally such a scripture conversation will lead individuals to an awareness of the need for some kind of action in response to what has been shared and learned. There may be no single answer or conclusion for everyone in the group. The scripture conversation should, however, strive to raise the consciousness of each person with respect to the issues addressed. This can be followed by a time for prayer in which individuals who wish to do so may share out of their personal experience.

USE OF ART

In a world increasingly oriented to various forms of entertainment and multimedia experiences, we might well explore the use of various art forms in our reflection on and praying of the scriptures. The dangers and limitations of such an approach will be obvious to those in parish ministry who have noticed that more and more of our people seem to come to church expecting to be entertained. Nevertheless, most of us have few opportunities to express the artistic part of ourselves, especially in relationship to the scriptures.

Choose a text such as those mentioned under "Guided Meditation" or any other text that involves rich imagery or potential for using the imagination. After the passage is read and briefly discussed, ask individuals or small groups to present its meaning through a drawing, skit, roleplay, or other form of creative expression. Ask the participants to include themselves in the picture, etc. What are we doing while Jesus prays? Do we identify with Mary or Martha? What is our relationship with others in the picture?

MUSIC

Ask members of a group to respond to a scripture story by means of musical expression. What type of music or particular piece of music is called forth in you by the passage? Or ask individuals to summarize their response to the passage by writing a single verse to fit the tune of a favorite hymn. A way of praying the scripture in this context might involve the writing of a second verse to express one's personal response to God after reflection on the text. Alternatively, if hymnals are available, ask the group to find a hymn that expresses what the scripture is saying.

HAIKU

Some groups may find it meaningful to respond to the experience of praying scripture by writing poetry. After a passage is read two or three times, give individual members of the group time to express the meaning of the passage or their own personal response to it in the form of a brief poem. Those who desire to do so may share their poems with the group.

   One form of poetry that may be especially well suited to such expression is the Japanese haiku, defined by the Haiku Society of America as an "unrhymed Japanese poem recording the essence of a moment keenly perceived, in which Nature is linked to human nature."[29] While the traditional form of the haiku was confined to three lines of five, seven, and five syllables respectively, many who write haiku in English are concerned less with the precise form and more with the ability of the poem to engage the reader with the feelings of the writer. The introduction of haiku in small groups may well lead individuals to continue their use as a disciplined means of responding to their personal praying of scripture. The following examples are by Kathrine Laycock:

Luke 1:46-55 [The Magnificat]
   To adore God
      and experience love returned.
   My yes is blessed!

Luke 2:41-51 [Jesus in the Temple at age 12]
   Now where has he gone—
      Acting like a child again.
   The Temple. But why?

Luke 4:1-13 [The temptation of Jesus]
   Gray wilderness road
      hot, dry wind—relentless blaze
   Tempted by mirage.

Luke 7:36-50 [Jesus at the home of Simon the Pharisee]
Sinful woman's gift—
ointment of tears and love.
"Your faith has saved you."

THE PREFACE
LUKE 1:1-4

. . . Because I have carefully studied all these matters
from their beginning, I thought it would be good to write
an orderly account for you.
(Luke 1:3, TEV)

THE PREFACE TO THE GOSPEL OF MARK consists of a single line, "This is the Good News about Jesus Christ, the Son of God," which readers often miss because of the way it blends into Mark's introduction of John the Baptist. Matthew's Gospel begins with a genealogical listing of the "ancestors of Jesus Christ" as a means of setting the birth narrative in some sort of historical context. The introduction to John's Gospel is theological in nature, probably adapted from an early poem or hymn.

The preface to Luke is unique among the four Gospels. Kodell describes it as, "like a memo clipped to a book manuscript, describing the book's contents and explaining why it has been written."[30] Acts, the second volume of Luke's work, begins with a similar "memo" that ties the two volumes together by summarizing the first and introducing the second. Although brief, Luke's preface serves as a dedication to Theophilus; describes his work in terms of his historical interest; and states his purpose for writing.

Luke seems to have been a student of history who wanted to approach his telling of the Christian story in an historical context. He acknowledges that others have "done their best" to report on the things that have happened. Then he describes his own purpose as that of providing "an orderly account," which meant a thoughtful consideration of the written sources already in circulation along with various other sources, probably including oral traditions. "I do this," Luke says to Theophilus, "so that you will know the full truth about everything you have been taught."

As will be noted in the commentary for the meditation on the preface, Theophilus was a common name in Luke's time and may represent an actual person. If so, Theophilus could have been a recent convert to Christianity as well as a person who functioned in some official capacity in the Roman Empire, perhaps in Antioch. If this was the case, it is possible that Theophilus may have been Luke's financial patron. On the other hand, it is possible that Luke took advantage of the name as a means of addressing his Gospel to all those who love God. In either case the Gospel was written to make available not just "an orderly account" but also "a fuller account" to those who are relatively recent converts to the Christian faith.

. . . So that you will know the full truth . . .

Commentary: Theophilus, meaning "lover of God," was a common name in the Greek world. Some have suggested that Luke wrote his Gospel to a specific person of that name, perhaps someone in a position of influence. While Luke does not say so, it is possible that Theophilus was his financial patron. It has also been suggested that, whether or not Luke had an actual person named Theophilus in mind, it may have been his way of addressing his Gospel to all who love God. The introduction recalls that "many people," some who were eyewitnesses and others who have since proclaimed the good news, have written about Jesus and his teachings. Luke, however, felt the need for "an orderly account" so that those who love God come to understand the full truth about what they have heard from other sources.

Preparation: Even a simple passage of scripture like this one can provide important insights for prayer, but only if we are fully present to it. Try to put other thoughts out of your mind for these few minutes and be open to hearing what God may have to say to you in these words.

Read 1:1-4: You are "a lover of God." Read this preface to the Gospel as if it were addressed to you personally.

Reflection: How do you feel being addressed as "Lover of God"? How do you feel about beginning an orderly reading and praying of Luke's Gospel? Even though you have read it many times before, what might it mean for you to "know the full truth about everything that you have been taught"? Are you ready to devote some time on a regular basis to this opportunity?

Prayer: Share with God your feelings as you begin this praying of Luke's Gospel. Ask for the guidance of the Spirit so that you may be open to a fuller understanding of what you have been taught.

THE BIRTH NARRATIVE
LUKE 1:5–2:52

Do not be afraid; for see—I am bringing you good news of great joy for
all the people: to you is born this day in the city of David a Savior, who
is the Messiah, the Lord.
(Luke 2:10-11, NRSV)

THE FIRST MAJOR SECTION OF LUKE'S GOSPEL is the magnificent
narrative relating to the birth and childhood of Jesus. It has been
called by many the prologue to the Gospel. There is a sense in
which it stands apart from the rest of the Gospel, leading to
speculation that it may have been a later addition. The theory is
supported by the presence in 3:1 of a typical prophetic
introduction which could well have constituted the original
opening of the Gospel. In addition, as most scholars point out, the
first two chapters constitute a clear and cohesive unit apart from
the rest of the Gospel. They also present a kind of summary in
advance of the Gospel as a whole. Some have argued that the
prologue was intended to parallel the Gospel as a whole, with the
final story of Jesus in the Temple at age twelve pointing to his
teaching ministry in the Temple just prior to the passion. Indeed,
these two chapters are best understood only after one is familiar
with the structure and flow of chapters 3 through 24.

Luke's account of the conception, birth, and childhood of
Jesus is apparently of his own creation. There is nothing similar in
Mark that could have provided a model for him. And while
Matthew also has a birth and infancy narrative, there is no
indication that either had any knowledge of the other's work. As
Kodell says, "they composed their accounts separately at a time
when the church was reflecting back beyond Jesus' public
ministry to his earthly beginnings."[31]

The structure of Luke's birth narrative is masterful in part
because of his parallel stories about John the Baptist and Jesus.
The annunciation stories are almost mirror images of one another:

the angel Gabriel appears to a parent (Zechariah and Mary), who responds with apprehension and fear; the angel reassures the parent and then announces the birth; an objection is raised and a sign is given. The names of both Jesus and John are given by the angel in advance; both Jesus and John are circumcised on the eighth day; and both Mary and Zechariah respond to the event with a canticle. Nevertheless, Luke makes it clear at every stage that Jesus and John are not of equal importance. Jesus is the fulfillment of God's promises, while John's role is that of forerunner to "prepare the way of the Lord."

How will I know if this is so?

Commentary: This is the first of two annunciation stories that open the first major section of the Gospel. The respective announcements to Zechariah and Mary regarding the coming births of John and Jesus both follow a pattern established in the Hebrew Bible for the birth of an important person (compare the birth of Isaac in Genesis 17):

1) an angel appears;
2) a troubled response on the part of the recipient;
3) reassurance is given and the birth is announced;
4) an objection is raised;
5) a confirming sign is given.

Note the parallelism between this passage and verses 26-38 that announce the birth of Jesus.

Preparation: The scene is the inner chamber of the Temple in Jerusalem. Imagine yourself as someone privileged to sit in a quiet corner and observe what is about to happen.

Read 1:5-22: Read the passage once to get a sense of the flow of the story; then go back and read it again, noting the elements mentioned in the introduction.

Reflection: Imagine yourself present with Zechariah as he went about his religious duties in the Temple. What were Zechariah's reactions to this event? What would your reactions be? Would your own skepticism also cause you to ask: "How shall I know if this is so?" Does this or a similar question occur to you when you read or hear about other promises of God? What would it take for you to be more trusting?

Prayer: Let your prayer begin with your reactions to this reading. Acknowledge to God any feeling you may have had. Ask God for the grace to recognize those times when "angels" appear to you, and for the grace to respond in faith and trust.

Now at last the Lord has helped me

Commentary: It is difficult for us to imagine the feelings of Elizabeth and Zechariah in whose time childlessness was considered a matter of disgrace. The inability to have children was always blamed on the woman and even constituted grounds for divorce. Under these circumstances it would have been easy for a person like Elizabeth to have become bitter, blaming God for her misfortune. Yet we have the impression that she remained faithful, bearing her "public disgrace" with dignity. Her response to the miraculous pregnancy, "Now at last the Lord has helped me," seems to suggest that, in spite of her advanced age, she had never given up hope.

Preparation: Praying scripture cannot be rushed. Decide that this is important enough to devote your full attention to for these few minutes . . . and then do it.

Read 1:23-25: Read this brief passage carefully, looking between the lines for more of Elizabeth's response.

Reflection: Can you imagine yourself in the place of Elizabeth, bearing the stigma of childlessness for so many years? How would you have felt? How would your relationship with God have been affected? What would your reaction have been when Zechariah came home, literally speechless, with the news? What might have been your reaction to the pregnancy? Do you remember the reaction of Sarah when Abraham gave her similar news? Is there something you have waited a long time for in your life that now seems almost beyond hope? How would you feel if it happened?

Prayer: Share with God your feelings about something you have long hoped for.

. . . May it happen to me as you have said

Commentary: While the essential elements of the two annunciations are parallel, there are important differences. The announcement to Zechariah took place in the Temple, the very center of Jewish life and worship. But the announcement to Mary occurs in a relatively unimportant town in the scorned province of Galilee. Zechariah was elderly, Mary very young. John will be "great before the Lord, but Jesus will be the "Son of the Most High God." Both Zechariah and Mary find their respective announcements difficult to believe. Mary is troubled, confused, and afraid. But her response is to believe, "for there is nothing God cannot do."

Preparation: Before you settle down to pray this passage, try a few seconds of gentle exercise to help release some of the tension present in your body.

Read 1:26-38: Take time to read this passage several times. Note the overall flow of the dialogue. Go back and listen to Mary's responses, not just her words, but her feelings.

Reflection: Can you put yourself in Mary's place as you reflect on this event? Of what does Mary's "blessedness" consist: her having been chosen by God? her faith? her willingness to accept this unexpected role? How do you feel about Gabriel's words, "there is nothing that God cannot do"? And what about Mary's response, "I am the Lord's servant, may it happen to me as you have said"? What have you felt God calling you to do? What is your response?

Prayer: Begin your prayer with the knowledge that "God has greatly blessed you." Give thanks for that blessing and open yourself to be "the Lord's servant."

Why should this great thing happen to me?

Commentary: Luke now proceeds to connect the two annunciation stories by telling of Mary's going to visit Elizabeth. This becomes yet another means of stressing the greatness of Jesus relative to John. Elizabeth is filled with joy and humility, and even the unborn John "jumped with gladness" within her! Elizabeth's statement, "How happy you are to believe that the Lord's message to you will come true," points to Mary's having been chosen to be the mother of the Lord and also to her acceptance of God's will in her life. Elizabeth's humbling of herself before Mary foreshadows John's later humbling himself before Jesus. Luke says that Mary remained in the home of Elizabeth and Zechariah for three months, apparently returning to her own home shortly before the birth of John.

Preparation: As you get ready to pray this or any scripture passage, pause long enough to take several long, slow, deep breaths. Hold each breath a few seconds and then let it out and, along with it, the remaining tension that may be present in your body.

Read 1:39-45: Read this brief account. Pause a moment or two before reading it a second time. This time, pause after each of Elizabeth's statements or questions.

Reflection: Note that there is no dialogue in this scene. The words all belong to Elizabeth who proclaims "blessed" both Mary and her special child. She appears to be overwhelmed that "my Lord's mother comes to visit me." How do you feel about the humility of Elizabeth's response, both to what has happened in her own pregnancy, and in her reaction to Mary's visit? Does Elizabeth's response call you to greater faith and to a willingness to accept the role you are called to play in the reign of God?

Prayer: Ask God to give you the grace of being able to respond with joy and humility at the faith of others.

LUKE 1:46-56 (NRSV)

My soul magnifies the Lord, and my spirit rejoices in God my Savior

Commentary: Mary's response to Elizabeth is one of the most beautiful canticles of the Bible. The *Magnificat,* as it is known from the first word of the Latin translation, is more than a joyous thanksgiving for what God has done for Mary. It is also Luke's announcement of what God *will* do for the world. Everything will be turned upside down, a process that has already begun with God's choice of a humble young woman to be the mother of the Messiah. The powerful will be brought down and the lowly lifted up; the hungry will be filled and the rich sent away empty. The text, which summarizes some of the major themes of Luke-Acts, is modeled on the Song of Hannah in 1 Samuel 2:1-10. This magnificent celebration of God's action is sung daily in the evening prayer office of many monastic traditions.

Preparation: If prayer and praying the scriptures is important, then it is worth preparing for. This must include the preparation of our bodies. Briefly take inventory of the tension in your body beginning with your feet and continuing up to your head. Consciously let go of the tension in every muscle group, including those around your forehead, eyes, and mouth.

Read 1:46-56: These beautiful words need to be read again and again. You may want to take time to read them in several different translations.

Reflection: The Magnificat has been called a radical statement of social justice. What do you think? What events in recent history reflect the bringing down of the powerful and the lifting up of the lowly? In an age when justice seems to be lacking in so many places, can you take heart in this affirmation that such things will happen?

Prayer: Sing this song again with Mary, praying with and for the poor and oppressed of our world.

What is this child going to be?

Commentary: Luke turns now to the birth, circumcision, and naming of John. The focus is on the naming, an act that carried much greater significance in biblical times than it does in our own. The angel's announcement to Zechariah, and the fact of Elizabeth's age and previous inability to have children have pointed toward the special nature of this child. Now he receives a special name. Friends and relatives expect him to be named after his father, as was the custom. But both Elizabeth and Zechariah insist that "his name is John," which means "gracious gift of God." Zechariah then regains the ability to speak, and those gathered for the occasion are "filled with fear" (awe) as they too realize that John is no ordinary child.

Preparation: The ability to be fully present to praying the scriptures can be greatly affected by our posture. While this may vary with each individual, most people find it helpful to sit with the feet flat on the floor, back straight, and the hands resting comfortably in the lap. Find the balance point for your head to avoid tension in the neck muscles.

Read 1:57-66: Read this passage, taking note of the elements of the story mentioned in the introduction above. Then, after a moment of silence, go back and read it again as you try to sense the feelings of those who were there.

Reflection: Imagine yourself among those present at the celebration of John's birth. There is unrestrained joy because of the special circumstances. That joy turns to awe and wonder as an unexpected name is confirmed by the miracle of Zechariah's regaining his ability to speak. Would you not also be among those who ask, "What is this child going to be?"

Prayer: In an age when so many children are homeless, poor, and abused, pray that more parents and other adults might be filled with awe at the birth and potential of every child.

You will go before the Lord to prepare the way

Commentary: Verse 67 introduces the *Benedictus,* a title that reflects the opening word of the Latin translation. This wonderful canticle is sung during the morning office of many monastic communities. It begins with a prophetic hymn praising God for fulfilling the ancient promise of a savior from the house of David. In verses 68-75 Luke has drawn upon numerous themes from the Hebrew scriptures, some of which are found in Psalms 34, 67, 103, and 113. The second part of the canticle, verses 76-79, speaks of the role of John as the one who will prepare the way of the Lord. Here Luke may have drawn his theme from Malachi 3:1-2, Isaiah 9:2, and 42:7. Verse 80 brings this passage to a close, locating a mature John in the desert where we will next encounter him shortly before the baptism of Jesus.

Preparation: Simple things like time, place, and attitude can make important differences in our ability to become centered for prayer. Have you tried different times of the day to discover which feels best for you?

Read 1:67-80: Like the Magnificat, this canticle deserves to be read several times and in different translations.

Reflection: Can you hear the unrestrained joy in the opening verses as Zechariah praises God for fulfilling the promise made to our spiritual ancestors long ago? God has "come to the help of his people and has set them free"! (TEV) And to what purpose? "So that we might be holy and righteous. . . all the days of our life"! (TEV) Read and reflect on the final magnificent sentence of the canticle, verses 78*b*-79. Zechariah more than made up for his inability to speak during the nine months of Elizabeth's pregnancy!

Prayer: Begin your prayer by reading once more (aloud if possible) verses 68-75 and 78-79. Continue with your own praise and thanksgiving.

There was no room for them to stay in the inn

Commentary: The tradition of the birth of Jesus is found only in Matthew and Luke and with significant differences concerning the details. Matthew implies that Mary and Joseph were residents of Bethlehem, while in Luke they come to Bethlehem from Nazareth in Galilee in order for Joseph to be enrolled in a census in his ancestral city. While Luke's details about the date of the census might ordinarily help to establish the year of Jesus' birth, in this case they are of no help because they do not agree with known dates of Roman enrollments. Apart from this introduction, Luke's account of the birth is extremely brief . . . only one sentence in the Greek text! Because all the guest rooms were filled, the parents-to-be chose the only available space, a stable, possibly one of the many caves in the hillside just below the town of Bethlehem.

Preparation: As it was important for Mary and Joseph to find a place to stay, it is important for us to find a place to pray. How do you feel about the place you have chosen for praying the scriptures? Is it free from distractions and interruptions?

Read 2:1-7: Read these brief verses first to refresh your memory about the content. Then, after a moment or two, go back and read them again, giving special attention to verses 4-7.

Reflection: If you have ever spent a whole day of your vacation driving toward your destination, only to get there and find a "no vacancy" sign on every motel, you may have some idea of the plight of Mary and Joseph. Add to that the fact that Mary was pregnant and about to deliver. Reflect on the words, "there was no room for them." Have you ever been in a situation where there was no room for you? What is the modern equivalent of the cave where Mary finally found rest?

Prayer: Pray for the homeless, the mentally ill, runaway children, and others in our society for whom there is "no room."

Do not be afraid

Commentary: Whereas the miraculous event following the birth of John was Zechariah's regaining the ability to speak, the miraculous event following Jesus' birth is the appearance of heavenly angels! The angel in verse 11 provides us with a summary of Luke's Christology, including the term *savior*, which was not used by either Matthew or Mark. Characteristic of Luke is the fact that the news comes first to a group of humble shepherds, not to kings as in Matthew.

Preparation: In most churches, the sanctuary, a word meaning "holy place," is a space set aside primarily or exclusively for prayer and worship. Can you find such a holy space for prayer in your home or elsewhere?

Read 2:8-15: Because it is such a prominent part of our Christmas Eve services, many Christians could come close to reciting this text from memory! Even so, read it now at least twice before going on to meditate on it.

Reflection: Numerous phrases in this text provide rich resources for meditation, but let us focus on four simple words spoken to the shepherds by the angel Gabriel: *Do not be afraid.* This phrase, or close variations of it, occurs at least one hundred times in the Bible, including nine in Luke. "Do not be afraid," the angel said to Zechariah, later to Mary, and now to the shepherds. Jesus will later use the same words in speaking to James and John, Jairus, and whole crowds. What are you afraid of right now? Can you hear the words, *do not be afraid* addressed directly to you in your situation?

Prayer: Share with God some of the fears in your life. Listen.

Mary treasured all these words and pondered them in her heart

Commentary: In the second half of this passage, the angels disappear and the excited and curious shepherds hurry off to Bethlehem to "see this thing that has happened." (One wonders who watched the sheep while they were away!) They are thus the first, not only to hear the news, but to visit the Christ child in Bethlehem, bringing news of the chorus of angels singing praise to God. In Bethlehem the responses are varied: all who heard were amazed; Mary pondered the news in her heart; and the shepherds went back to their waiting sheep, glorifying and praising God.

Preparation: Perhaps you use a candle, an icon, or some other object to help define your "holy space." Making it a simple place free of clutter can help you free your mind of its own clutter as you center yourself for prayer.

Read 2:16-20: Read this brief passage slowly; then after a moment or two go back and read it again, pausing long enough after each verse to visualize in your mind the action suggested.

Reflection: *Pondering* is one of those words that may sound a little old-fashioned to our modern ears. It means to think deeply about something or to meditate. It may be that it sounds old-fashioned to us because in our busy lives we seldom take the time to do it— at least not consciously. Yet, we all daydream, which is a kind of pondering. Perhaps what we need to do is to recover the art of pondering. Sitting in a comfortable chair before a cozy fire is a wonderful way to ponder. Sitting in church is often a good way to ponder. Christmas Eve is a very special time to ponder the same questions Mary pondered sitting in a stable.

Prayer: Take time now to ponder something that is important to you. Allow God to listen in.

This child is chosen by God for the destruction and the salvation of many

Commentary: In the opening verses of this section Luke combines the observance of two Jewish laws. The first required that every firstborn son be presented to the Lord (Exod. 13:2, 12-16), and the second called for the ritual purification of a woman forty days following childbirth (Lev. 12:1-8). The visit to the Temple to fulfill these laws becomes the occasion for two remarkable testimonies to the identity of Jesus as the Messiah. The first is that of Simeon, described by Luke as "a God-fearing man," who was "waiting for Israel to be saved." The canticle of Simeon proclaims Jesus as "a light to reveal [God's] will to the Gentiles." His later statement to Mary provides yet another preview of Luke's message: that Jesus will be the cause of much controversy and that Mary, herself, will suffer much because of him.

Preparation: Prayer demands the full attention of our minds and bodies. Things like a full stomach or a recent cup of coffee can interfere with your ability to become centered.

Read 2:21-35: Read this passage, noting the purposes for the visit to the Temple. After a moment, go back and read verses 25-35 again, picturing the old man, Simeon, as he takes the little child in his arms, gives thanks to God, blesses the parents, and delivers his painful message to Mary.

Reflection: Simeon in his prophetic witness proclaims that Jesus has been chosen by God "for the destruction and the salvation of many in Israel." There will be nothing lukewarm about the Messiah. Nearly every encounter he will have with individuals and groups will be a time of confrontation. Everyone who comes into contact with him will have to say yes or no to him.

Prayer: Ask God to be present with you as you continue to pray Luke's Gospel, knowing that over and over again your own encounters with Jesus and his teachings will call for a yes or a no.

Day and night she worshiped God

Commentary: This passage continues with the appearance at the "very same hour" of an old prophetess named Anna. The Greek text is ambiguous as to whether she was eighty-four years old or had been a widow for eighty-four years. In any case she, like Simeon, represents the faithful of Israel. Her witness complements that of Simeon and carries it even farther by spreading the news to others who were "waiting for Israel to be saved."

Preparation: Are you worried about something you have to do? Are you feeling rushed about the rest of the day or evening? If your prayer time is important, it is worth consciously putting those things aside for these few minutes. You can resume worrying later! For now, allow your mind, body, and spirit to be fully devoted to the practice of prayer.

Read 2:36-38: Read the entire passage (verses 22-38) to set the context; then after a moment or two go back and read again the three brief verses about the witness of Anna.

Reflection: Luke tells us that Anna "never left the Temple; day and night she worshiped God, fasting and praying." What image forms in your mind of this woman? In our time many might regard her as an eccentric whose religious devotion had been carried to an extreme. Yet in the Israel of her time she would have been revered, both for her age and because she was a prophetess. Perhaps she, like Simeon, took the child in her arms and blessed him. Perhaps she also spoke prophetic words to Mary and Joseph. Whatever details have been left out of the story, we know that Anna became the first public witness about this special child.

Prayer: Pray for those aged saints in our time who witness quietly to their faith, and that you may also possess this grace when you reach the age of Anna.

LUKE 2:39-52 (NRSV)

All who heard him were amazed at his understanding

Commentary: Verses 39-40 conclude Luke's birth narrative and turn our attention to the mature Jesus. Luke, to our delight, adds a story not found in the other Gospels. It begins with the annual pilgrimage to Jerusalem for the Passover Festival. Because Jewish law required even those living at some distance to attend the festival, it would be natural for a large crowd of family, friends, and neighbors to travel together and for Mary and Joseph to assume that Jesus was somewhere in the company. When they discovered him missing, they hastily returned to Jerusalem, where they found him sitting in the Temple discussing theology with the elders! Up to this point others have proclaimed Jesus' special nature. But here, in his response to his worried parents, Jesus proclaims the meaning of his own life. The story of the young Samuel at Shiloh is the prototype for this story.

Preparation: This reading mentions the amazement of people because Jesus seemed so intelligent for a twelve-year-old boy. We need to learn more about the scripture intellectually. But we also need to pray it in order to seek God, to experience God's presence, and to discover God's will for our lives.

Read 2:39-52: Read this story of the boy Jesus. Then read it a second time with attention to the feelings of Mary and Joseph and to the reaction of those in the Temple to the precocious Jesus.

Reflection: Jesus' parents are "astonished" when they see and hear him engaged in discussion with the Jewish teachers. Perhaps their astonishment was more at his boldness than at his knowledge, since they must have been aware of that already. Luke describes the reaction of others who heard Jesus, using a phrase that he will use again in other situations: "All who heard him were amazed." We too are amazed at his insight and wisdom, even after many readings of the Gospels.

Prayer: Ask God to turn your amazement at Jesus into a deeper understanding of who he is and who he calls you to be.

THE PREPARATION NARRATIVE
LUKE 3:1–4:13

After all the people had been baptized, Jesus also was baptized. While he was praying, heaven was opened, and the Holy Spirit came down upon him in bodily form like a dove. And a voice came from heaven, "You are my own dear Son. I am pleased with you."
(Luke 3:21-22, TEV)

IF THE OPENING OF MARK'S GOSPEL is dramatic because of its economy of words, Luke's is dramatic both for its double opening and the detail provided by its narrative. While Mark covers the ministry of John the Baptist, the baptism, and the temptation of Jesus in only thirteen verses, Luke expands the same material to fifty-one verses, including the addition of a genealogy of Jesus.

This "preparation narrative" consists of four distinct units: 1) the ministry of John, son of Zechariah (Luke doesn't refer to him as "John the Baptist" until 7:20); 2) the baptism of Jesus; 3) the genealogy of Jesus; and 4) the temptation of Jesus in the wilderness. Together these introduce the reader to the immediate background and preparation for Jesus' mission as it will be presented in the remainder of the Gospel.

Scholars have long puzzled over the relationship of this preparation narrative to the earlier birth and infancy narrative, often called the prologue to the Gospel. Some have argued that the Gospel originally began with the classic historical introduction found in 3:1-2 and was later expanded to include the birth and infancy narrative. The brevity of the historical introduction to the birth narrative (1:5a) has been cited as evidence for the later addition. The theory seems at least plausible enough, but the fact remains that no early text of Luke has ever been found that does not include the birth narrative.

However the two narratives came into being, each plays a distinctive role at the beginning of the Gospel. While the first serves to identify Jesus' divine nature in relation to his human origins, the latter offers a perspective on Jesus in relationship to current political history (3:1-2); current prophetic history (3:3-22); biblical history (3:23-38); and Israel's classic struggle with evil (4:1-13).

What then should we do?

Commentary: The next major section of Luke's Gospel opens with the story of John the Baptist. Following a pattern established in the Hebrew scriptures, John's prophetic ministry is introduced by setting it in historical context. Next Luke sets the scene in the desert, a reminder of the place where Israel's covenant relationship with God began. John's purpose as the forerunner is established by the quotation from Isaiah which Luke extends to include the vision of universal salvation, a major theme of his Gospel. John preaches repentance from sin, saying that those who do not turn away from their sins will be like trees that are "cut down and thrown into the fire" because they do not bear good fruit. Next Luke's theology of social responsibility is presented in response to three groups who ask John, "What then should we do?" Luke closes this section by making it clear that the Messiah is not John, but rather, someone who is coming.

Preparation: John's preaching, like many other biblical events, took place in the desert, always a place of testing. There is a very positive sense in which our prayer takes place in the desert, where, stripped of all pretense, we come before God ready to hear what we are often unable to hear in other circumstances.

Read 3:1-20: This is a relatively long passage with many possibilities for our praying. Read it slowly, carefully. . . at least twice.

Reflection: In the desert we are more open to reflect on the meaning of our own lives and our relationship with God. We have all had such desert experiences, often related to a change of pace and scene. Allow yourself time to be in the desert with John and those who came to hear him. Listen to the question, "What then should we do?" as it is asked by three different groups. Listen to John's answers.

Prayer: Ask the question for yourself, "What then should I do?" Allow God to help you understand what in your life needs to be turned around in order for you to bear good fruit.

The Holy Spirit descended upon him

Commentary: For those familiar with the more detailed accounts of Jesus' baptism in Matthew and John, Luke's version seems all too brief. He refrains from describing the baptism in order to call our attention to the opening of heaven and the manifestation of the Holy Spirit. Even Luke's description of heaven being opened pales in comparison with Mark, who speaks of the heavens as *torn apart.* (This may be a literary frame which will find its counterpart when the curtain of the Temple is torn in two with Jesus' death on the cross.) Luke's purpose is clearly to emphasize the presence of the Spirit, symbolized in the descending dove. The voice from heaven proclaims, in words borrowed from Psalm 2:7 and Isaiah 42:1, "You are my own dear Son. I am pleased with you." The Spirit empowers Jesus for ministry, which will begin immediately following his temptation. Note that in Luke, unlike the other Gospels, this event happens while Jesus was praying.

Preparation: Distractions, always distractions. Don't feel alone if you have difficulty focusing on your prayer without drifting off to completely unrelated matters. We all have the same problem. But we can learn to focus more and more on the matter of prayer.

Read 3:21-22: You may want to read the more detailed accounts of Matthew and John for comparison. Then come back and note the clear intention of Luke to focus on the coming of the Spirit.

Reflection: Luke's brief quotations from Psalm 2 and Isaiah 42 point not only to Jesus' special relationship with God, but to the kind of Messiah Jesus will become, namely a servant. We will hear this sign repeated in the voice from the cloud at the Transfiguration (chapter 9). What do you make of Luke's presentation of this event in the context of Jesus' praying? Watch for other similar occasions in Luke's Gospel.

Prayer: Pray that your own prayer life might be such that you are open to receiving the Spirit of God in special ways, even those ways we might ordinarily dismiss or not notice at all.

He was the son of . . .

Commentary: Biblical scholars have proposed various theories for Luke's inclusion of a genealogy and for his inserting it at this point in his Gospel rather than at the beginning as Matthew did. As Eugene LaVerdiere has pointed out, "Luke both affirms and denies Joseph's parentage of Jesus."[32] The parenthetical statement in verse 23 that Jesus "was the son, so people thought, of Joseph," acknowledges Joseph as the legal father, but also reminds us of the annunciation. In so doing Luke places Jesus firmly in the context of biblical history while, theologically speaking, affirming him as the son of God. While Matthew's genealogy traces Jesus' ancestry back to Abraham, Luke goes all the way back to Adam, thus including all humankind in Jesus' ministry, not just the descendants of Abraham.

Preparation: Our minds are terribly undisciplined, wandering from one thought to another several times every minute. But, by accepting this human limitation, we can begin to become more disciplined in our ability to focus on prayer.

Read 3:23-38: This is one of the few Lucan passages for which a single reading is sufficient!

Reflection: For those of us with an interest in genealogy, such a passage is at least intriguing. As any genealogist will recognize, the line of descent was designed by Luke, not for historical accuracy, but for theological purposes. It is similar to our claiming to be of "English descent," when we know very well that some of our ancestors were also Scandinavian, German, Irish, Huguenot, etc. While the persons named in Luke's genealogy are not necessarily the physical ancestors of Jesus, they represent his theological heritage. The bottom line is that Jesus is, as the final words of this passage state, the "son of God."

Prayer: Have a conversation with God about your genealogy. What are your national and cultural roots? And beyond that, whose daughter or son are you really?

Jesus was led by the Spirit into the wilderness

Commentary: While the word *temptation* often reminds us of weakness, it comes from a Latin word that means "to stretch" or "to try the strength of something." If the baptism of Jesus was for the purpose of empowering him for his ministry, then the temptation experience that followed immediately was to try his strength, further preparing him for what lay ahead. In the Hebrew scriptures the wilderness is traditionally a place of testing. Presumably Jesus' experience took place in the Wilderness of Judea, a large area stretching eastward from Jerusalem down to the Jordan Valley and the Dead Sea. It is a semi-arid region of hills and canyons inhabited mainly by wild animals. It was an ideal place for solitude and reflection. The Hebrew word for *forty* also means "a long time," and recalls the forty-year testing of the Israelites on their Exodus journey through the wilderness. The powers of good and evil are present with Jesus in the form of the Spirit and the Devil. By his answers to the three temptations, all quotations from Deuteronomy, Jesus refuses to usurp the power of God, seek political power, or claim exemption from human vulnerability.

Preparation: There is a sense in which Christian prayer is always an entering into the wilderness to "try our strength."

Read 4:1-13: Read the section, noting especially verses 1-2 and 13. In your second reading, focus on the three temptations.

Reflection: How do you feel about Luke's statement that Jesus "was led by the Spirit" into the wilderness? Do you think of the wilderness as something negative or as a place free of distractions where you can experience a positive encounter with the powers of good and evil? Jesus' answer to temptation in each case came from the scripture. What might be the role of scripture in those times when your own strength is tried?

Prayer: Ask God to help you experience wilderness as a positive opportunity for spiritual stretching and growing.

JESUS' MINISTRY IN GALILEE
LUKE 4:14–9:50

Then Jesus, filled with the power of the Spirit, returned to Galilee, and a report about him spread through all the surrounding country. He began to teach in their synagogues and was praised by everyone.
Luke 4:14-15 (NRSV)

BY FAR THE LARGEST PART OF THE GOSPEL, beginning with 4:14 and continuing through chapter 21, is devoted to the teaching, preaching, and healing ministry of Jesus. This material is divided into three sections based largely on geographical considerations. These sections are usually known as 1) the ministry in Galilee; 2) the journey to Jerusalem; and 3) the ministry in Jerusalem prior to the passion narrative.

Luke himself seems to have thought of Jesus' ministry in much the same way. The beginning and ending of the Galilee section are clearly drawn to our attention in the text itself. At 4:14, immediately following the account of Jesus' temptation in the wilderness of Judea, Luke says, "Then Jesus, filled with the power of the Spirit, returned to Galilee. . . ." He likewise calls attention to the conclusion of Galilean ministry by saying in 9:51, "When the days drew near for him to be taken up, he set his face to go to Jerusalem."

With two possible exceptions, all of the events in this section take place in the province of Galilee. One is the story of the healing of the Gerasene demoniac (8:26-39), which occurred in Gentile territory southeast of Lake Galilee. The other is the account of the Transfiguration and related events which, according to parallel accounts in Mark and Matthew, may have taken place north of Galilee around Caesarea Philippi.

Luke's narrative locates the beginning of Jesus' ministry in Galilee alone. He preaches in his hometown synagogue in Nazareth as well as in other towns, including Capernaum. Later he calls his disciples, teaches, heals, exorcises demons, and engages in controversy with those in the religious establishment.

Beyond the brief summary in 4:14-15, Luke firmly grounds Jesus' ministry in the prophetic tradition with the account of his reading and preaching from Isaiah in the synagogue at Nazareth:

> *The Spirit of the Lord is upon me,*
>   *because he has anointed me*
>   *to bring good news to the poor.*
> *He has sent me to proclaim release to the captives*
>   *and recovery of sight to the blind,*
>   *to let the oppressed go free,*
>   *to proclaim the year of the Lord's favor.*
>   (4:18-19, NRSV)

In the reactions of the people of Nazareth, Luke foreshadows the ultimate response to Jesus' ministry and its conclusion in Jerusalem.

The time has come

Commentary: Verses 14-15 serve as a transition from Judea to Galilee. They also inform us that the power of the Holy Spirit that came upon Jesus at his baptism remains with him, a theme that will be reinforced once more when Jesus preaches in Nazareth. Finally, Luke reminds us that Jesus is thoroughly rooted in the tradition of the synagogue, which for adult males meant taking one's turn reading from the Torah or the Prophets. Jesus, returning to his hometown, may have been honored with an invitation to read. The passage, from one of the servant songs of Isaiah, became a way of stating the nature of Jesus' role as Messiah. In his comment, Jesus announces that there will be no more waiting for the time when God will save the people. That time is today, and Jesus himself is the instrument of fulfillment.

Preparation: One thing. That is the goal, learning how to focus your attention on *one* thing rather than many. It can be a repeated phrase (mantra), a visual object, a sound, counting your breaths, or whatever helps you to focus on *one* thing rather than constantly drifting from one to another.

Read 4:14-21: Read verses 14-21. The rest of this section will be the focus of another meditation.

Reflection: By identifying himself with Isaiah's vision of the Messiah, Jesus announces that salvation is not just a spiritual matter; it also has a social dimension. Furthermore, the end of oppression is no longer something to be hoped for in the future. "The time has come" (verse 19). "Today this scripture has been fulfilled" (verse 21, NRSV). *Now* is the time! For the Christian there can be no politics that delay justice; no economics that allow oppression; and no law that sets one standard for criminals on the street and another for criminals in government. Compare this passage from Isaiah with Luke 1:51-55.

Prayer: Ask God to help you understand your role in a faith which proclaims that "now is the time for oppression to end."

A prophet is never welcomed in his home town

Commentary: Jesus' appearance in the synagogue at Nazareth evoked a variety of responses. At first the people were "well impressed with him" and "marveled at [his] eloquent words." But then in his commentary Jesus quoted two proverbs which, in effect, called their attention to their own prejudice against foreigners. The illustrative stories from Elijah and Elisha draw our attention to a prominent theme of Luke, that Jesus' ministry is to be directed not just to the people of Israel, but to Gentiles as well. There was apparently some resentment among the people of Nazareth because of all the time Jesus had spent in Capernaum, a town they looked down upon because of its sizable non-Jewish population. And so their reaction turned to anger, and they responded by running Jesus out of town!

Preparation: Choose your one thing carefully and stick with it for a while, rather than turning too soon to something else. Whatever it is, simply keep coming back to it when your mind drifts away, as it inevitably will.

Read 4:22-30: First, read the entire episode beginning with verse 16. Then after a brief reflection, go back and read verses 22-30, which focus on the reaction of the people of Nazareth to Jesus' ministry to Gentiles.

Reflection: The people of Nazareth, like people everywhere, were the victims of xenophobia, an irrational fear of foreigners. How ironic that their reaction came as a result of hearing stories from their own scriptures! Was not the unconscionable internment of Japanese Americans during World War II the result of a similar xenophobia? While we prefer to think of our own generation as more enlightened, there is plenty of evidence to suggest that xenophobia still plays a part in our individual and collective response to people who are different from ourselves.

Prayer: Pray for an increased awareness of your own irrational fear of foreigners and for God's help in overcoming it.

What do you want with us, Jesus of Nazareth?

Commentary: The scene now shifts to Capernaum on the north shore of Lake Galilee, which became Jesus' headquarters for his ministry in Galilee. Luke, following Mark, has already mentioned Capernaum in 4:23. The discrepancy is not important, because in Luke chronology is often sacrificed for the sake of theology. In Capernaum the power of the Holy Spirit with Jesus since his baptism is demonstrated in numerous healings, one of which is the man with the evil spirit in the synagogue. The belief in such spirits (or demons) had entered Judaism through contact with other religions and provided a convenient, though not universal, explanation for various physical and mental conditions. Craddock makes the important point that "in the Gospels the influence of demons is physical or mental, not moral."[33]

Preparation: You will be distracted in your effort to focus on one thing. That's just the way our undisciplined minds function. Gently allow distracting thoughts to drift away. You can come back to them later if need be. Now is the time for prayer.

Read 4:31-37: Read this passage first to sense the scene and the action; then read it again, noting especially the question of the man in verse 34 and the questions of the witnesses in verse 36.

Reflection: The question in verse 34 seems to be asked, not by the man himself, but by the evil spirit in him on behalf of the whole realm of evil spirits. It is the recognition of the power of good by the power of evil. Whatever we in modern times may think about evil spirits, we still have to contend with such forces in our own human condition. Do we not experience the same question whenever our greed, jealousy, selfishness, etc., are challenged by the teachings of Jesus? "What do you want with us?" The answer, if we take it seriously, calls for change in who we are.

Prayer: Reflect for a moment on your own sins and shortcomings. Allow them to ask the question, "What do you want with us, Jesus of Nazareth?" Open yourself to hear the answer.

LUKE 4:38-41 (TEV)

They knew he was the Messiah

Commentary: The home of Simon's mother-in-law was literally just a stone's throw from the synagogue in Capernaum. A combination of archaeological and biblical evidence suggests that this house served as the headquarters for Jesus' ministry in Galilee. It is here that Luke continues his references to Jesus' healing, not only of Simon's mother-in-law, but of others "who were sick with various diseases." By not naming those present, Luke assumes that we have read the details in Mark. Luke's emphasis is on the healings and on the fact that the demons recognized Jesus as the Son of God.

Preparation: When you have relaxed the tension in your body and begun to clear your mind of distractions, remember that God is always present in you, and that now you are simply entering into a fuller consciousness of that presence.

Read 4:38-41: Read this story first in Mark (1:29-34). Then read Luke's version.

Reflection: What do you think Luke is saying to us when he says that demons went out of many people, screaming, "You are the Son of God"? Take time to identify some of the "demons" that are a part of your own personality. What happens when your own demons get out of control in your anger, self-righteousness, pride, etc.? How do you feel when such things happen—guilty, ashamed, sorry, humble? In such moments do you have a heightened awareness of the power of good calling to you? Do you resolve not to make the same mistakes again? If so, perhaps you need to give thanks for the demons in you that help you to recognize the Son of God.

Prayer: Ask God to use even your "demons" to help you in your journey toward spiritual maturity.

At daybreak Jesus went off to a deserted place

Commentary: Having given us a preview of Jesus' healing ministry, Luke now moves on to highlight his preaching ministry. But these three verses also provide us with other insights. Whereas the people of Nazareth had run Jesus out of town, the people of Capernaum came running after him begging him to stay! Luke's statement in verse 44 that Jesus preached "in the synagogues of Judea" probably should not be taken to mean that he went south out of Galilee. "Judea" was sometimes used with reference to Palestine as a whole (Luke 1:5, Acts 10:37). But let us not overlook the opening sentence which tells us that Jesus, perhaps alone, got up early in the morning and went to a deserted place.

Preparation: Do you have regular times of quiet in your life when you can get away from other people . . . daily . . . weekly?

Read 4:42-44: Read this brief section once; then go back and read it again, noting all the different bits of information Luke has included in it.

Reflection: This brief passage tells us nothing about where Jesus went so early in the morning. Nor are we told whether or not he was alone. Still it is one of several places in the Gospels that speak of Jesus going off to a "lonely" or "deserted" place. Was it for prayer? Was it to deal with the temptations he may have felt as a result of his sudden popularity? How often do you take time to go to such a place to reflect on what is happening in your life? Do you need to do that more regularly?

Prayer: Ask God to help you find regular opportunities for solitude and reflection.

LUKE 5:1-11 (NRSV)

Yet if you say so

Commentary: Gennesaret, the name of the fertile plain just south of Capernaum, is Luke's name for what the other Gospel writers call Lake Galilee. Also unique to Luke is the later placement of the calling of the disciples, which seems more natural, coming in response to Jesus' growing popularity and preaching (here called for the first time "the word of God"). The crowd, large enough to force Jesus to preach from a boat, seems to disappear after verse 3, when our attention is turned to the fishing story. The focus is clearly on Simon, now already called Peter, with James and John in the background and Simon's brother Andrew not even mentioned. Obviously these fishermen were doing more than washing their nets (verse 2). They were also listening to Jesus' preaching, which, together with the sign of the large catch of fish, was enough to cause them to leave everything and follow him.

Preparation: Why do you pray? Is it because you feel obligated to pray, or because you feel guilty if you don't? If such feelings are part of your motivation, you might want to take some time to think them through and find a better reason for praying.

Read 5:1-11: As you read, note the details mentioned above. Then, after a moment, go back and read it a second time, imagining the scene and its impact upon Peter, James, and John.

Reflection: Can you put yourself in Simon's place and imagine this event happening to you? What is your reaction to the crowd and to Jesus' preaching as you wash your nets after a night of fishing? How do you feel about Jesus commandeering your boat for a pulpit? How do you feel when he tells you to continue fishing, when you know the fishing is best at night? Are you sufficiently moved by what you see and hear that you can say with Simon, "if you say so"? What is your response when you bring up a huge catch in your net? And how do you respond to Jesus' challenge to leave it all behind and follow him?

Prayer: Let your prayer flow out of your reaction to this story.

[84]

If you want to, you can cure me

Commentary: *Leprosy* was a term that included several skin diseases of the time. These were feared, not only because of their wasting effects on the body, but because one who suffered from such a disease was considered ritually unclean, unable to participate in communal worship. Such persons were ostracized by friends, neighbors, and even their own family. In this reading a leper humbles himself before Jesus, begging for help. His faith is demonstrated by his statement, "If you want to, you can cure me". . . in other words, if you are willing to touch me. Jesus did heal him and sent him off to the priest to be examined according to the procedures outlined in Leviticus 13–14, so that he might once again be integrated into society. Note the final verse, in which Luke again points out the balance between Jesus' public ministry and his withdrawal for reflection and prayer.

Preparation: As you get ready to pray a particular passage of scripture, you may find yourself less than enthusiastic about the material in it. Remember that it is just such readings that often surprise us with a new insight!

Read 5:12-16: After reading this story the first time, go back and read it again, taking time to form an image of the scene in your mind as if you were there as a witness to what happened.

Reflection: Remember a time when someone approached you on the street asking for help. Perhaps the person looked dirty or mentally deranged. Perhaps he or she asked you for money. What was your reaction? What emotions went through you? Compassion? Anger? Fear? Pity? Embarrassment? What did you do? How did you feel afterward? What do you think the person who approached you was feeling? Could he or she have been thinking, "If you want to, you can cure (or help) me"?

Prayer: Pray for greater sensitivity to those who suffer from poverty, disease, or social stigma. Ask God to show you a better way to respond to them.

Your sins are forgiven, my friend

Commentary: Although Luke follows the Marcan outline of the healing of the paralyzed man, he emphasizes the growing popularity of Jesus' ministry by adding the comment that the Pharisees and teachers of the Law, "had come from every town in Galilee and Judea and from Jerusalem." The story is appealing because those who wanted to see their friend healed were so determined that they went to the trouble of opening a hole in the roof to place him in the presence of Jesus. As some scholars have pointed out, Jesus' dual action in first forgiving the man's sins and then healing his paralysis is not necessarily an indication that Jesus saw the paralysis as psychosomatic. It may be that our tendency to think of ourselves as made up of body, intellect, spirit, and feelings prevents us from understanding Jesus' ministry to the whole person.

Preparation: As you prepare to read and pray this story, remember a time when you felt God's forgiveness for some sin in your life.

Read 5:17-26: As you read, try to put yourself in the scene, imagining yourself as one of those inside the house watching the events unfold. Then read it a second time, trying to identify with those who carried their friend to be healed.

Reflection: Who did you most strongly identify with as you read this story? What do you think was in the hearts of those who opened up the roof and let their friend down in front of Jesus? How do you feel about Jesus' double action in first forgiving the man his sins and then healing his illness? Does the sin in your life affect the way you feel mentally or physically? If so, what can you do about it?

Prayer: Share with God any personal feelings you may have as you have reflected on this story of forgiveness and healing. What would you like God to do for you today?

[86]

I have come to call not the righteous but sinners

Commentary: Levi's calling is the first of four incidents that bring Jesus into conflict with the scribes and Pharisees. His instant and decisive response is striking, perhaps indicating a growing relationship with Jesus over a period of time. Yet that is not the real purpose of the story. While Simon described himself as "a sinful man" when Jesus called him (5:8), Luke now makes the point that Jesus' call is meant even for those whose sin is a matter of public knowledge! The complaint about Jesus associating with sinners is answered in the form of a proverb: "Those who are well have no need of a physician, but those who are sick." The idea is extended to a new metaphor when Jesus says, "I have come to call not the righteous but sinners to repentance."

Preparation: If the need to pray arises out of our love for God, then it makes no difference whether we see ourselves as righteous or sinful. In either case our need is to pray.

Read 5:27-32: In your first reading put yourself in the place of the scribes and Pharisees, scandalized by Jesus' eating and drinking with sinners. Then, read it again from Levi's perspective.

Reflection: That, "the church is not a museum for saints, but a hospital for sinners" is a modern version of the proverb quoted by Jesus, addressing the need of those both inside and outside the church. The New Revised Standard Version emphasizes the spiritual condition of the individual when it says, "I have come to call not the righteous but sinners to repentance." But the Today's English Version calls attention to another dimension of Jesus' ministry by saying, "I have not come to call respectable people to repent, but outcasts." Those who are "sinners" must often bear the additional burden of the social stigma placed upon them by the reaction of others. Where do you see yourself on the continuum of righteous person or sinner?

Prayer: Ask God to help you better understand who is called by Jesus and why.

New wine must be put into fresh wineskins

Commentary: Luke, like Mark, does not clearly identify those who ask why Jesus' disciples ate and drank while others observed the laws about fasting twice a week. Perhaps it was some of those attending Levi's banquet. The real intent of the question has to do with the new spirit of joy and celebration that surrounded the activities of Jesus in contrast with the air of strictness that characterized the scribes and Pharisees. For Luke, Jesus represented a new way of looking at things, welcoming those shunned as sinners by the leaders of traditional Judaism. His disciples were common people whose response to this new freedom was celebration rather than asceticism. The passage addresses not just the new way of being religious, but also the difficulty the traditionalists had trying to understand Jesus. The metaphors used by Jesus to explain this phenomenon are much like our saying, "you can't teach an old dog new tricks."

Preparation: Before preparing yourself to read and pray this passage, try to remember the difficulty you sometimes experience in understanding or accepting something that may seem new or radical by your own standards.

Read 5:33-39: Read these verses to get a sense of what is being said. Pause to reflect on the meaning of the metaphors about an old coat and old wineskins. As you read it a second time, try to sense the feeling of those who asked the question.

Reflection: As most of us grow older we may find it difficult to give up accustomed patterns of thinking and acting. Thus we may be offended by those who make light of something we take very seriously. Do you remember your parents or grandparents shaking their heads over your new ideas? Can you think of ways in which you ought to "lighten up"? Are there parts of your own spirituality that need to be less serious and more joyful?

Prayer: Ask God to help you better understand your reactions and those of others to the ways of Jesus.

Why are you doing what is not lawful on the sabbath?

Commentary: The conflict between Jesus and the Jewish leaders continues with questions about what is or is not permitted on the sabbath. In the first instance the Pharisees accuse the disciples of picking and eating grain on the sabbath, which was technically against the laws having to do with harvesting. Jesus' answer takes the position that human needs, in this case being hungry, may take precedence over such laws. He cites the example of David being allowed to eat bread from a shrine that was normally reserved for use by the priests. Luke's inclusion of this question quite likely reflects discussions that were taking place in the early church for which he was writing. Some in the church wanted to remain faithful to the Jewish Law, while others felt free to move in new directions. Luke's answer means that while the church is not free to ignore Jewish Law altogether, it must be interpreted in light of Jesus, who is the Lord of the sabbath.

Preparation: While there is much to be said for the discipline of praying scripture at a regular time every day, the spirit of today's reading should remind us that there may be occasions when our human needs are such that it is better to postpone our prayer until a time when we can be fully present to it.

Read 6:1-5: As you read, take time to let yourself imagine the scene and listen to the dialogue.

Reflection: Most of us pride ourselves in being "law-abiding citizens." Yet, we sometimes "bend the rules" to fit the need of the moment and quite properly so. Stop signs and traffic lights serve an important purpose, providing a structure that allows traffic to move with at least some degree of order. Yet who would disagree with the man who cautiously ignores a stop sign in order to get his wife to the hospital in time to deliver her baby? Can you think of times when you have chosen to ignore a law, tradition, or custom? What circumstances led to your decision?

Prayer: Explore with God your own feelings about laws.

LUKE 6:6-11 (TEV)

Some Pharisees wanted a reason to accuse
Jesus of doing wrong

Commentary: The conflict between Jesus and the Jewish leaders continues with the added intensity that those who oppose him are now actively looking for a reason to accuse him. The setting is in a synagogue where Jesus is teaching on the sabbath. Knowing what the scribes and Pharisees are thinking, Jesus asks the question himself in a way that puts the focus on the meaning of the sabbath. The implied answer is that not doing the good that can be done, even on the sabbath, would be an act of evil in itself. His opponents either do not understand what he is saying or, if they do understand, do not agree with him. They make no attempt to answer. Thus Jesus answers the question himself, by healing the man with the paralyzed hand.

Preparation: How much time do you allow yourself for praying these scripture passages? Do you feel rushed? If so, what can you do about it?

Read 6:6-11: Read the passage twice to gain an overview of what will happen in it. Then, imagine the scene in your mind. Who is there? How does the action flow? Read it again.

Reflection: Can you identify with the scribes and Pharisees in the reading? Have you even been mistrustful or angry at someone to the point of hoping that he or she would do something wrong? What was your reaction when someone did do something you disapproved of? What do you think of Jesus' question asking us why we would refrain from doing something good? If an opportunity presented itself for you to perform an act of genuine goodness for a person in need, under what circumstances might you want to refrain from doing it?

Prayer: Continue your reflection on these questions as you consciously allow God to "listen in." Do the questions change? Do your answers change? What do you hear God saying to you?

He called his disciples and chose twelve of them

Commentary: With the words, "Now during those days" (NRSV) or "At that time" (TEV), Luke temporarily sets aside the conflict between Jesus and the scribes and Pharisees in order to return to the earlier emphasis on the beginning of Jesus' ministry and its growing popularity. Following a night alone in prayer, Jesus calls his disciples together and "selected twelve of them" (NAB) whom he named apostles, meaning those who are "sent out." This name is important for Luke, who uses it sixty times in his Gospel and in Acts to distinguish the "twelve" from other disciples of Jesus. The number twelve suggests the twelve tribes of Israel.

Preparation: Becoming "centered" and ready to read and pray will differ with each individual. Nevertheless, we need to avoid the temptation to abbreviate the steps that work best for us just because we feel the pressure of time.

Read 6:12-16: This reading is brief yet deserves our full attention and reflective reading. Spend some time with individual phrases of the first two verses. Then pause to remember something about some of the apostles named.

Reflection: Again, Luke calls attention to Jesus' taking time away from the crowds to pray, even a whole night. How many of us would spend more than a few minutes praying about something that will happen the next day? Are we not more likely to spend the night in restless sleep, rather than praying? If you took time to reflect on the names of Jesus' apostles and their backgrounds, you may have been struck by the fact that they were all very ordinary people. As such they will often misunderstand Jesus, wish he were a different kind of Messiah, and otherwise fumble their way to Jerusalem where they will deny him and flee into hiding. But later they will understand and bring the church into being. If God can use such as these, there is surely hope for us!

Prayer: Give thanks to God for these special people "sent out" by Jesus, every one of them an ordinary person just like you.

LUKE 6:17-19 (NRSV)

All in the crowd were trying to touch him

Commentary: In verses 17-19 the scene shifts as Jesus moves down from the mountain to "a level place" where a large crowd gathers to hear him and to be healed. This level place, or "plain" as it is often known from the King James Version, is the setting for Luke's version of the sermon that begins with the beatitudes. Present are three groups: the apostles, the rest of the disciples, and the people. In saying that the latter had come from all over Judea, from Jerusalem and from Tyre and Sidon, Luke seems to be saying that Jesus' message is for everyone, including the Gentiles. The power that came to Jesus at his baptism continues to come "out from him" (NRSV) to heal the people.

Preparation: How do you feel about the contrast between the quiet reflective time you spend praying scripture and the pace of your schedule the rest of the day?

Read 6:17-19: Reading these three verses, imagine the scene with the apostles, a large number of disciples, and a crowd of people from all over. Where would you place yourself in this crowd?

Reflection: If you have ever been in a large crowd gathered around a well-known political leader, sports figure, or entertainer, you have some sense of the scene in Luke's "level place." But there is another dimension. Jesus was not just another "hero." He spoke as the Gospels say, "with authority," offering a fresh new perspective on theological questions. He brought hope and joy to a religious climate that had become dull and oppressive. And there was more. Through the power of the Holy Spirit, he brought healing. For all these reasons the people thronged around him, hoping to be healed or transformed by the power of his touch. Can you place yourself in this scene? How would you like to be changed by the power of Jesus' presence or perhaps even by his touch?

Prayer: Open yourself to be touched by the power of God's spirit working within you.

Blessed are you

Commentary: Even though there are important differences in the presentation of the beatitudes by Matthew and Luke, it is generally assumed that they were derived from a common source. While Matthew's blessings are addressed in the third person, Luke's are addressed directly to the disciples of Jesus. And Luke's blessings, while fewer in number, are matched with a parallel set of woes. As such they are intended, not as suggestions for how to be happy or how to avoid being unhappy, but as announcements of the way life is experienced inside, as opposed to outside, the reign of God.

Preparation: As you settle down and prepare yourself to pray the scriptures, be mindful of the fact that you are not alone. Thousands of people all around the world are praying with you.

Read 6:20-26: Read these verses, conscious of the fact that they are addressed not just to Christians in general, but to you. As you read them a second time, try reading the corresponding "blessings" and "woes" together (verses 20, 24; 21, 25; 22, 26).

Reflection: The New Revised Standard Version, New English Bible, New American Bible, etc. translate the Greek word *makarioi* as "blessed" or "blest," while others such as Today's English Version and the Jerusalem Bible have chosen the word "happy." One New Testament scholar, Professor Robert H. Gundry, suggests that the meaning becomes more clear if we substitute the word, "congratulations!"[34] This carries the sense of rejoicing with someone who has been very fortunate (in the sense of God's approval, rather than the human understanding of *fortunate*). Congratulations, you who are poor. In the realm of God, the ordinary values of the world are turned upside down! You will get more out of life than those who are rich! What are the values that have been turned upside down in your life? Congratulations!

Prayer: Ask God to help you better understand the joy of life as it is envisioned in the beatitudes.

Love your enemies

Commentary: Here is the heart of the gospel, the radical love that is the mark of the Christian. It is a way of life counter to what our human nature suggests. Yet it is by living these "upside-down" values that we become children of God. Verses 27-31 establish the principle that those who follow the way of Jesus do not reciprocate the behavior of those who would victimize them. Nor do they adopt a "victim mentality." Rather they respond as God responds to them . . . with love, kindness, and mercy. Verses 32-36 repeat the principle, arguing that it should not be applied only to those who are kind and loving. How radical is this love? As Jerome Kodell says, "Even the Golden Rule perched in the middle of these verses seems tinny against such a dazzling standard.[35] Verses 37-38 offer a fitting reminder of God's generosity.

Preparation: Before praying this passage try to recall a recent incident in which you felt mistreated or insulted by someone.

Read 6:27-38: Read verses 27-31; pause a moment or two and then read the same verses again; then after another brief pause read verses 32-38.

Reflection: How many times have we thought of these words simply as "an ideal to strive for"? Yet Jesus proposes this kind of radical love not as a matter of philosophical curiosity, but as the standard by which his followers are to live! Our human condition makes this difficult to comprehend. When someone insults us, our reaction is instantaneous and is often felt physically. We become angry and want to strike back. But the bottom line is still, "No! Love your enemies and do good to them." Surely this is something that we cannot learn simply by thinking about it. We have to *do* it. Only by the repeated discipline of responding with love in real life situations can we hope to retrain ourselves.

Prayer: In your prayer, take inventory of your own ability to love your enemies, confessing your failures and asking God for the grace to grow toward the kind of love you have been shown.

First take the log out of your own eye

Commentary: Verses 39-42 draw on two images of the human eye and our ability or inability to see. The first is about literal blindness, while the second speaks of being blind to one's own faults. Luke may have combined these images from different sources. In Matthew Jesus uses the first image to criticize the leadership of the Pharisees (15:14) and the second to prepare the twelve apostles for their mission (10:24-25). In the last two verses of the present reading Jesus uses both humor and hyperbole to make the point that none of us has the right to criticize others, because we are unable to recognize our own faults.

Preparation: Praise, adoration, petition, and confession are among our many reasons for needing to pray. Today we are reminded of another . . . our own humility as we remember that we judge the faults of others as readily as we overlook our own.

Read 6:39-42: Verses 39-40 and 41-42 look at two different kinds of human blindness. You may want to focus on one in your meditation now and come back to the second at another time.

Reflection: Who among us has not had the experience of criticizing the faults of another person, only to have someone else remind us of a similar fault of our own that we have overlooked? If we are honest with ourselves the experience is not only embarrassing, but deeply humbling. As counselors sometimes point out, many of us have a tendency to criticize others for faults we don't want to face in ourselves. Take some time to reflect on the "log in your own eye." What in your own personality have you lived with so long that you are seldom aware of it? What is it in your personality that others see that you no longer see? What could you do about it?

Prayer: Confess to God one or more of your own faults that get in the way of your being more understanding of others. Ask for help in being more open about it with yourself and others.

The mouth speaks what the heart is full of

Commentary: The comparison of a tree and the fruit it bears is common to Matthew and Luke. Matthew, in fact, uses it twice (7:16-20 and 12:33-35). By placing it immediately after the illustration about those who see the speck in someone else's eye, but fail to see the log in their own eye, Luke seems to be underscoring that point. Such hypocrisy is easily perceived by others. As Fred Craddock says, this passage points out the shallowness of the popular expression, "it's not what you say but what you do that counts."[36] For Luke, even what you say points others to the reality of who you are.

Preparation: In order to set your time for prayer apart from the other activities of the day, you might want to establish a symbolic ritual to mark the special nature of this time. It can be as simple as lighting and blowing out a candle or perhaps taking the phone off the hook.

Read 6:43-45: After reading these verses for the first time, take a moment to recall one or two people who might serve as examples of the mouth speaking what the heart is full of. Then read the passage a second time.

Reflection: If our bodies are full of things like cholesterol, pesticides, preservatives, and carcinogens, we cannot be physically healthy. If our minds are filled with negative thoughts, self-pity, and half-truths, then we cannot be mentally healthy. In this passage Jesus asks us to look at what our hearts are full of. Some hearts are clearly filled with joy and peace. Others just as clearly are filled with anger, bitterness, guilt, and jealousy. Whatever is in our hearts will also be on our lips . . . more often than we realize. What do you think your heart is filled with? What would your friends, neighbors, and co-workers say your heart is filled with? What would God say your heart is filled with?

Prayer: Ask God to help you know your own heart.

Why do you call me, "Lord, Lord," and yet don't do what I tell you?

Commentary: Luke's story of the two house builders may not be as familiar to us as Matthew's version, in which the houses are built on rock and sand, respectively. It may be that the two stories were adapted to fit the experience of two different audiences. Matthew's version reflects the Palestinian terrain, where one could build a house on exposed rock. Luke's version, on the other hand reflects the physical terrain of his readers in Asia Minor, where one would have to dig to reach bedrock. But in either case the point is the same. Just as it is foolish to build a house not suited for local conditions, so it is foolish to profess belief in Jesus without living accordingly.

Preparation: Take time to set aside anything else you are doing so that you can give complete attention to the scripture and your praying it.

Read 6:46-49: Begin by reading Matthew's version (7:24-27). Then, after a brief pause, read it in Luke.

Reflection: In our desire to follow the teachings and example of Jesus most of us find some parts of the gospel that are relatively easy to follow in our own lives. Other parts are more difficult, yet possible for us. But there are others that for one reason or another we find very hard to follow, even though we believe they reflect the proper way for us to live. Reflecting on the image of the houses built on different foundations may be helpful. If someone asked you to describe the "foundation" of your life, how would you answer? What is it that is rock-solid for you? What is it that will stand up against the storms life may send your way? What in your life has not been able to weather the storms? What could you do to make your life more solid?

Prayer: Be honest with God about the foundations of your life. Ask for help in making needed improvements.

LUKE 7:1-10 (NRSV)

Not even in Israel have I found such faith

Commentary: A geographical change marks the end of the "sermon on the plain." As Jesus enters Capernaum the focus changes to his mission to the Gentiles, already alluded to when he preached in Nazareth. Here his first encounter is with a Roman centurion whose beloved servant is sick and near death. Note that the centurion has no personal contact with Jesus, choosing to communicate through two groups of intermediaries, one Jewish and the other presumably Gentile. This may be Luke's way of saying that his Gentile readers are at no disadvantage when it comes to the availability of Jesus' ministry. The Roman centurion is presented as a good and compassionate man who is close to and respected by Jews. Perhaps he was a believer, but not officially a Jew. In any case he recognized that entering the home of a Gentile would have made Jesus ritually unclean. Thus he sent the second delegation to say that it would not be necessary for Jesus to come, implying that Jesus' power to heal was just as effective even without his presence.

Preparation: What mood do you bring to your prayer today? How will it effect your ability to be fully present to the reading?

Read 7:1-10: Read the story slowly for perspective. Then read it again, even more slowly, being open to hear "between the lines."

Reflection: Luke's description of the Roman officer leads us to admire and respect him. He cares about his servant. He cares about his Jewish friends and even built their synagogue. He is sensitive to the religious customs that could put Jesus at an inconvenience. He is both humble and a man of faith. Have you met such a person who was otherwise a "Gentile" to you . . . perhaps someone of another faith or nationality? Such encounters remind us of God's universal love and our own provincialism.

Prayer: Pray that you may be even more open to those who come from other lands, adhere to a different faith, or otherwise hold views unlike your own.

A great prophet has appeared among us!

Commentary: The raising of the widow's son is unique to Luke. It seems to be modeled on the raising of another widow's son by the prophet Elijah in 1 Kings 17. Luke inserts it at this point in the Gospel in preparation for the statement in the next section (found also in Matthew) that "the dead are raised to life," which is part of Jesus' answer to the question by the disciples of John the Baptist. The story is simply told. The initial focus is on Jesus' compassion for the woman who has lost her only son. In the brevity of the story, the crowd that accompanied Jesus and those participating in the funeral are momentarily forgotten. They return in verse 16 filled with fear, praising God, and saying, "A great prophet has appeared among us!" and "God has come to save his people." The reference to Jesus as a prophet should not be understood, as some suggest, as a criticism of Judaism's failure to accept Jesus as anything more than a prophet. Nor should it be used to denigrate the role of prophet or otherwise neglect the vital role played by prophets in the Jewish tradition.

Preparation: If taking the time to center yourself is helpful in preparing for prayer, you might find it helpful to pause briefly at other times in your busy day to take some deep breaths and momentarily let go of the stress that fills your mind and body.

Read 7:11-17: Read these seven verses to become familiar with their flow. Then pause a moment to "set the scene" in your mind before reading them a second time.

Reflection: With whom did you identify in this story? If you were part of the crowd, was it the crowd following Jesus or the crowd of mourners? Would your reaction have been similar to or different from the reaction of the crowds in the story? Would your recognition of Jesus as prophet come only as a result of such a dramatic event? Do we recognize who Jesus is in less dramatic happenings?

Prayer: Let your reflection on this story flow into your prayer.

How happy are those who have no doubts about me!

Commentary: Although the four Gospels sometimes emphasize different or even conflicting details, most of us create our own version based on a combination of two or more accounts. For example, we forget that only in the fourth Gospel does John the Baptist identify Jesus as the expected Messiah. With this in mind, the question asked by John's disciples makes more sense. For Luke, who has already identified Jesus as the Messiah, their question provides an opportunity to elaborate what *kind* of Messiah Jesus is. While John believed the Messiah would come to be judge of the world (3:15-17), Jesus' answer in verse 22 points to his role as previously outlined in his sermon at Nazareth. He goes on to point out that some, like the tax collectors, had accepted John's preaching, while others, notably the Pharisees and scribes, had not. The proverb about children in the market place makes the point that the Jewish leaders accepted neither Jesus nor John. This is reinforced in verses 33-34, reflecting the strict table customs of the time. These will be dramatized in the following passage.

Preparation: As you ready yourself to pray this reading, recall some of your own questions about what kind of messiah Jesus is.

Read 7:18-35: Both the length and the subtle issues raised in this passage require that it be read at least twice.

Reflection: John's preconceived idea of the Messiah seems to have caused confusion in his mind about who Jesus was. The scribes and Pharisees also held images of the Messiah that got in the way of their accepting Jesus, not to mention the hang-ups they had over things like regulations about table fellowship. Do you have images about who Jesus *should be* that get in the way of your understanding his role as he defined it himself? What are they?

Prayer: Ask God to help you clear away your own preconceptions about Jesus in order to better understand who and what he really is.

The great love she has shown proves that her many sins have been forgiven

Commentary: The similarities of this story and those in Matthew 26:6-13, Mark 14:3-9, and John 12:1-8 suggest a common origin. Yet there are important differences. In Luke and John the woman anoints Jesus' feet; in Matthew and Mark it is his head. Luke seems to set the story in Galilee, while the other Gospels all place it in Bethany. John has it in the home of Mary, Martha, and Lazarus. The synoptics have it in the home of Simon. The approaching death of Jesus is the focus in Matthew, Mark, and John, while Luke adapts it for his own purpose. For those who may wonder what this woman who leads a sinful life was doing in the house of a Pharisee, A. E. Harvey suggests that the occasion was a formal dinner party which often attracted visitors who came to beg for scraps of food or simply to hear the conversation.[37] When Simon wonders why Jesus allows the unclean woman to touch him, Jesus, knowing both Simon's mind and the character of the woman, tells a story about two men who owed money to a moneylender, ending with a question for his host. Simon's cautious answer allows Jesus to compare Simon's meager hospitality with the woman's gratefulness. The point is not that the woman was forgiven because of her love, but that her love was a result of her being forgiven.

Preparation: One way to prepare for prayer is to spend a few moments remembering a favorite place where you felt completely relaxed and at peace.

Read 7:36-50: This powerful story deserves our full attention. Read it several times to gain a sense of the place and the action.

Reflection: Close your eyes and imagine yourself present at the table when the woman enters and begins to wash Jesus' feet. What do you see? What do you feel? What do you want to say?

Prayer: Enter into a conversation with God about this story and your reactions to it.

[101]

And many other women

Commentary: Like many people in the Gospels, the woman in the foregoing story remains anonymous. But who is to say she was not among those "many other women" now mentioned by Luke who followed Jesus and "used their own resources" to help him? While it would be a mistake to ascribe modern feminist qualities to Luke, he does seem to have been much more sensitive to the needs and roles of women than other Gospel writers. It hardly seems a coincidence that the uniquely Lukan material contains back-to-back stories emphasizing men and women. The story of the good Samaritan is followed by the story of Mary and Martha. The parables of the lost coin and the lost son focus on a woman, then men. The parable of the widow and the judge is followed by the parable of the Pharisee and the tax collector. At least some of the women who followed Jesus had been healed of diseases (verse 2). But some must have followed him for other reasons. Women were clearly among the many who supported Jesus, not only financially, but in other ways, to the very end. These women were, as one of Jesus' followers says in 24:22, part of "our group." If only we knew more about their stories!

Preparation: How would you feel if you suddenly found a particular reading to be so rich that you needed more time to reflect on it? Would you have the time? Would you take the time?

Read 8:1-3: These three verses seem relatively uncomplicated. But read them as you would any other passage.

Reflection: Why do you think Luke included these verses? Go back and read them again. Who do you think these "other women" were? What do you think Luke means in saying that they "used their own resources to help Jesus and his disciples"? Remember as you continue reading and praying Luke's Gospel to be sensitive to the way he mentions women.

Prayer: Share with God your reflections on these verses and ask for insight into Luke's view of women and their role in ministry.

Knowledge . . . comes by means of parables

Commentary: Luke now begins a unit drawing our attention to the word of God and the importance of our hearing it. In 5:36 and 6:39 he has already used the term *parable* to introduce brief illustrations in Jesus' teaching. But it is only with the "Parable of the Sower" that we encounter a parable in the fuller sense of the word. C. H. Dodd defines the special nature of the parable:

> At its simplest, the parable is a metaphor or simile drawn from nature or common life, arresting the hearer by its vividness or strangeness, and leaving the mind in sufficient doubt about its precise application to tease it into active thought.[38]

In parables the hearer is invited to become a participant, providing his or her own interpretations. Even the traditional titles are subjective. Is this the parable of the sower, the parable of the seed, or the parable of the soils? Should it be the parable of the prodigal son or the parable of the forgiving father? To discover what a parable means we must let go of our need for rational explanations and allow our minds be teased.

Preparation: Take a moment to remember your childhood or some other time when hearing stories was important to you.

Read 8:4-10: Read verses 4-8 and take time to reflect on the parable itself (which will be more fully explored in the next meditation). Then read verses 9-10 before continuing.

Reflection: Do you remember stories that began with phrases like, "Once upon a time" or "Long, long ago and far, far away"? Can you reflect on this parable without looking for intellectual explanations? Communicating with stories is rare in our western culture, as you will discover if you try to tell someone a story rather than "explain what you mean."

Prayer: Ask God to help you relax enough to enjoy communicating through parables.

[103]

Those who hear . . . but

Commentary: The interpretation of this parable turns it into an allegory, with each detail representing a person or condition. However, the interpretation becomes awkward when the scattered seed is identified both with "the word of God" and "those who hear" the word. Perhaps the parable might be easier to understand had the Gospel writers not included the interpretation! On the other hand, the problem serves to illustrate the point made in the commentary on verses 4-10, that the parable is an art form to which the listener/reader is invited to bring his or her own interpretation. This parable most likely reflects the varied responses to the church's early missionary efforts under various conditions.

Preparation: Take a few moments to reflect on the question: "Who is God for me at this point in my life?" If the question seems to require extra time, feel free to postpone your meditation on the reading until another time.

Read 8:11-15: You may want to go back and read verses 4-8 and proceed directly to a time of reflection on them. Then return to read the interpretation in verses 11-15 and reflect on them as well.

Reflection: While we have all heard interpretations of this parable that allude to different responses to the word of God on the part of different people, it may be helpful to take another approach this time. Read through verses 4-8 again with the thought of the seed (the word of God) all being sown within you personally. Ask yourself what the path represents in your own personality. What in you is the rocky ground lacking moisture? What are the thorn bushes in you that choke the word? And what is the good soil in you?

Prayer: Give thanks to God for this parable that allows you to examine your own spirituality. Ask God to help you rework those things inside you that condition how you hear and respond to the word.

Be careful, then, how you listen

Commentary: Luke's unit on the importance of hearing the word of God closes with three independent sayings, all of which will be found later in other contexts (11:33, 12:2, and 19:26). The first uses the analogy of a lamp to make the point that God's word is not meant to be hidden, but to give light. The second assures us that Jesus came not to hide the truth of God but to bring it out into the open where we can learn from it. The third saying is more challenging, especially for those inclined to hear it in material terms and thus think of it as unfair! The meaning here is that those who are spiritually attuned and seeking to grow will do so by attentiveness to parables, while others will profit little because their pride, stubbornness, etc., keeps them from being open.

Preparation: What attitude do you bring to reading and praying the scriptures? Do you look forward to each experience or are you doubtful about your growing through this process?

Read 8:16-18: Each of these three verses is a separate saying. It would be well to read and reflect on each before going on to the next.

Reflection: How do you feel about the first saying? Is it reassuring to hear that God's word is like a lamp that is not hidden away, but placed out in the open so we can use it? How about the second saying? Have you had the experience of reading a particular passage of scripture many times, thinking you understand it, only to discover something in it later that you had missed before? Even though the word is out in the open like a lamp, we may not always see it right away! This insight leads to the truth of the third saying, cautioning us to be careful how we listen. The attitude and experience we bring to our hearing and reflecting on the word can make all the difference in our ability to receive even that which is "out in the open."

Prayer: Have a conversation with God about the attitudes you bring to your reading, praying, and reflecting on the scripture.

My mother and brothers are those who hear the word of God and do it

Commentary: While Matthew and Luke sometimes followed the same order and context found in Mark, in other instances they adapted Mark's material to fit their own purposes. This included abbreviation and change of context, as we see in this passage. The parallel story in Mark is set in the midst of a controversy with some scribes who had come from Jerusalem. It also implies a degree of controversy within Jesus' own family (Mark 3:21ff). But there is no such controversy in Luke's telling. Instead he chose to let the incident involving Jesus' mother and brothers illustrate what he had previously said about hearing and obeying the word of God. The important thing for Luke is the family of God, and members of that family are "those who *hear* the word of God and *do* it."

Preparation: When you are ready to read and pray these verses, pause a moment or two to imagine a scene where Jesus is teaching in the midst of a crowd. His mother and brothers are on the edge of the crowd, unable to get closer to him.

Read 8:19-21: Read the three verses. Pause. Recall the scene in your mind. Then read them a second time.

Reflection: Have you ever stood on the edge of a crowd wishing for the opportunity to be the next speaker so you could ask a question or share your own ideas? Those of us who are introverts may recall a time in school when we wanted to answer the teacher's question, but didn't put our hand up because we were shy. How do you suppose Mary and her sons felt in this situation? There is not the slightest hint of Jesus being impatient with his family when someone calls attention to their presence. In Luke's context his answer might even be understood as a high compliment to his mother and brothers.

Prayer: Ask God to help you to open both your spirit and your ears so that you may hear the word and do it.

Where is your faith?

Commentary: The story about Jesus calming the storm is unusual in the sense that it occurs when Jesus is alone with his disciples, who are thus the recipients of Jesus' power rather than simply witnesses, as is most often the case. While the story no doubt has roots in a real life situation (sudden storms are common on Lake Galilee), it is likely that Luke uses it also in a symbolic sense. By crossing the lake Jesus and his disciples were moving from Jewish to Gentile territory. Notice also that Jesus is about to send the disciples out on their own (9:1-6). These factors alone would be enough to create a storm of fear and doubt in the hearts of the twelve. It should also be remembered that Luke is speaking to the early church, which had plenty of stormy experiences of its own that called for reassurance of Jesus' calming presence.

Preparation: Remember a time in your own life when you saw a heavy storm approaching, watched it as it passed through the place where you were and then began to fade in the distance. Remember the sense of relief and peace you felt afterward.

Read 8:22-25: Do something different! Read Psalm 29, which describes how a powerful storm approaching northern Israel from the Mediterranean is deflected to the south by Mt. Hermon, then turned to the west by dry desert air, so that it goes back out to the sea. Notice the "voice of the Lord" in the thunder. After a pause, read Luke 8:22-25.

Reflection: Can you recall a time when some situation in your life caused you to react with fear and panic as the disciples do in this story? What did you do? What happened? How did you feel in the "calm after the storm"? How do you respond now to the storms that sometimes pass through your life? "Where," in all this, "is your faith?"

Prayer: Give thanks for the calming presence of God when storms hit your life. Ask for a deeper faith to meet the storms that will continue to come.

Jesus, . . . What do you want with me?

Commentary: That the journey across the lake was a journey into Gentile territory is confirmed by the details of the healing story that follows. Luke and Mark give the location as the "territory of Gerasa," which is unlikely since that town was located in the mountains thirty miles southeast of the lake. Other manuscripts (and Matthew) call the place Gadara, which was still several miles away, but at least within sight of the lake. In either case it was Gentile territory, as other details of the story attest. The healing of the man with the many demons follows the pattern of an exorcism which might in itself have been newsworthy. But it seems likely that those who came to see what had happened were also thinking about what happened to the pigs. Indeed, as Craddock suggests, their fear and request for Jesus to "go away" may have had more to do with the economic implications of the loss of so many pigs than with the healing of the man with whom they were obviously acquainted.[39] Jesus' asking the man to stay home and witness to "what God has done for you" is Luke's way of underscoring the importance of the mission to the Gentiles.

Preparation: If there is something troubling you, give yourself permission to "put it on the shelf" while you pray. It will still be there when you are ready to take it up again.

Read 8:26-39: This passage contains numerous interesting details that shed light on the story as a whole. It deserves to be read slowly and carefully . . . at least twice.

Reflection: What was your reaction after you read this story the first time? Did anything about it trouble you? What questions does it raise for you? Take time to reflect on them. What do you think of the man's question, "Jesus, Son of the Most High God! What do you want with me?" The NRSV says, "What have you to do with me?" Have you ever wanted to ask the same question?

Prayer: Allow yourself to ask God the question, "what do you want with me?"

She . . . touched the edge of his cloak

Commentary: In the previous story about the Gerasene demoniac Luke has again made the point that Jesus' ministry extends to Gentiles, even those who raise pigs! Now back "on the other [western] side of the lake," Jesus has returned to Jewish territory, as the details of the healing of the woman with the hemorrhage and the raising of Jairus's daughter clearly indicate. In this story within a story the central figures are both "unclean," one because of the nature of her illness and the other because of the prohibition about touching the bodies of the dead.

Preparation: Before you get ready to read and pray, reflect for a moment or two about the power of human touch.

Read 8:40-56: Begin by reading the two stories separately. First read the story of Jairus's daughter in verses 40-42*a* and 49-56. Then read the story of the woman with the hemorrhage in 42*b*-48. Now go back and read them together as Luke presents them.

Reflection: *The Oxford English Dictionary* devotes more space to the word *touch* than any other word in the English language. Some dictionaries may have as many as twenty-five or more definitions for *touch* as a noun and several more when it is used as a verb! Human beings have many ways of touching one another. Scientists tell us that our skin as a sensory organ contains as many as six hundred "receptors" per square inch. All together there are more than 500,000 receptors which relay important messages from our skin to our brains. These serve not only to distinguish hot from cold and pain from pleasure, but to convey feelings and emotions such as love, friendship, faith, and hope. As the two stories in this reading indicate, there is far more power in human touch than most of us realize. Take a few moments to reflect on the power of touch in your own experience.

Prayer: Give thanks for the power of human touch, for the many ways in which your life has been touched by God, and for the power you have to touch other people for good.

[109]

Take nothing with you . . . .

Commentary: Luke has already defined "the twelve" as *apostles* meaning, "those sent out" (6:12-16). Now the time has come for them to go out on their own to exorcise demons, heal the sick, and preach the reign of God. In order to keep them focused on their mission, Jesus instructs them to take nothing with them, "no walking stick, no beggar's bag, no food, no money, not even an extra shirt." Just as there are to be no props or no distractions, they are to be completely dependent upon the hospitality of people they meet along the way. Thus they will be free, not just to preach, but to live by the values of God's reign. By asking them to shake the dust off their sandals against those who would not receive them, Jesus was not suggesting an act of hostility, but a warning to those who cut themselves off from salvation by their unwillingness to hear the gospel.

Preparation: Remember a special place where you once experienced a genuine sense of wholeness and peace. Allow yourself to be there again . . . feeling the peace.

Read 9:1-6: Read these six verses first to get a sense of the scene and the action. Then read them a second time, giving your attention to the specific instructions Jesus gave to the apostles.

Reflection: Imagine yourself as one of those being sent out by Jesus. What would you feel as he gave you authority to drive out demons and cure diseases? How would you feel about being asked to preach the reign of God? Finally, in an age when we "pack everything but the kitchen sink," how do you feel about Jesus' instruction to "take nothing with you"? Can you imagine going even on an overnight trip under such conditions? What would it be like? How would you feel, depending completely on others for hospitality? How would the message you carried to others be different because you took nothing with you?

Prayer: Ask God to help you understand what your reflections on this reading might be saying to you.

Who is this about whom I hear such things?

Commentary: Luke has made us well aware of Jesus' growing popularity. The fact that large crowds gathered and followed him everywhere was bound to draw the attention of political leaders, including Herod Antipas, the ruler of Galilee. The resentment of the people against Roman domination and taxation gave Herod good reason to keep track of Jesus' activities. He would have been worried about those who saw in Jesus the possibility of political revolution. Speculation about Jesus' identity was widespread, making it understandable that Herod would also wonder who he was. Although this is Luke's only reference to the death of John the Baptist, some were saying that Jesus was John the Baptist resurrected. Others thought that, in Jesus, Elijah had reappeared or that another ancient prophet had come to life again.

Preparation: Before you pray this scripture, pause to ask yourself the question: "Who was Jesus, really?"

Read 9:7-9: After reading these verses once, read them a second time, trying to put yourself in the position of Herod Antipas, ruler of Galilee.

Reflection: The question of Jesus' identity has already been raised and will be raised again shortly in 9:18-22. It was a question on the minds of his disciples, his followers, politicians like Herod Antipas, and others who encountered him along the way. It is a question that consumed great amounts of energy in the early church and is still debated in our own time. Who was Jesus? What exactly was his relationship to God? We can imagine Herod's interest in finding an answer to this question. What about you? How do you answer the question for yourself? What facts are important to you: his teachings, his miracles, his power to heal, the response of others around him?

Prayer: Be open in your prayer about any questions you may have about who Jesus was. Ask God to help you find new answers to those questions.

They all ate and had enough

Commentary: Luke now comes back to the mission of the apostles. The opening sentences prepare us to hear what might be called a debriefing after the apostles' return. But the planned retreat in the hometown of Philip, Andrew, and Peter (John 1:44) is interrupted by yet another crowd. The remote location and the lateness of the hour are cause for two questions: what are all these people going to eat and where are they going to sleep? When some disciples suggest sending the people away to find food and lodging, Jesus says, "You yourselves give them something to eat." What follows is a demonstration of "the theology of enough" in contrast to the economics of scarcity. Jesus organizes the crowd into small groups where sharing becomes both possible and natural. Then, out from under their cloaks, come the provisions people would obviously have brought with them to a remote area. The result: "They all ate and had enough." Interruptions can be occasions for continuing ministry. Earlier versions of this story undoubtedly influenced the development of the eucharistic liturgy of the early church including the four actions of taking, blessing, breaking, and giving.

Preparation: Ask yourself how you would feel if right now your phone rang or someone came to your door with a request, interrupting your time of prayer. How would you respond?

Read 9:10-17: There is a lot in these eight verses. You may want to read them several times, each time giving particular attention to something mentioned in the commentary above.

Reflection: Remember a time when you suddenly had unexpected company just before mealtime. If it was one of those times when there wasn't much in the kitchen, what did you do? Did you function out of an economics of scarcity . . . or a theology of enough? How did you feel when your guest(s) came unexpectedly? How did you feel later? What is hospitality?

Prayer: Ask God to help you to learn the "theology of enough."

One day when . . .

Commentary:

"One day Jesus was standing on the shore . . . "(5:1)
"One day when Jesus was teaching . . . "(5:17)
"One day Jesus got into a boat . . . "(8:22)
"One day when many tax collectors . . . "(15:1)
"One day when Jesus was in the Temple teaching . . . "(20:1)
Luke's frequent use of phrases like, "one day when" to introduce new sections may sometimes cause the reader to gloss over what follows! In this instance it is a reference to Jesus' praying, which in Luke almost always signals us that something important will follow (compare: 3:21; 6:12; 9:29; 11:1, and 22:44). Here Jesus prays before asking his disciples the question already asked by Herod and by the disciples themselves (8:25 and 9:9). Peter's answer, "You are God's Messiah," prepares the way for the verses that immediately follow, when Jesus begins to teach the disciples what kind of Messiah he is.

Preparation: Remember a time when you were especially fervent in prayer because of some event or question that was looming on the horizon of your life.

Read 9:18-20: Read these three verses; pause; then read Matthew's version of Peter's declaration (Matt. 16:13-17).

Reflection: Who does Herod Antipas believe Jesus is? Who, according to reports, do others say Jesus is? Who does Peter say Jesus is? Who do you say Jesus is? If your answer is the same as Peter's answer, then the next question is, what kind of a Messiah is Jesus? How do you answer that question?

Prayer: Ask God to help you better understand who Jesus is and what that means for you and for the world.

Those who want to save their life . . .

Commentary: Even for those closest to Jesus it was difficult to understand what kind of Messiah he was. He told them he would suffer and be put to death but three days later would rise to life. Those who believe he is the Messiah, he said, must be prepared to follow him. Verses 24-26 contain three parallel sayings of a proverbial quality. Those who would follow him must be willing to give up the values taught by the world in order to live by the upside-down values of God's reign. Put another way, one may gain happiness and success by the world's standards and still be spiritually empty. Notice that Luke's phrasing of verse 27 carries a different emphasis than the parallels in Matthew 16:28 and Mark 9:1. While Luke does not deny a *future* fulfillment of the reign of God, those who are able to follow Jesus can experience it here and now.

Preparation: Before you center yourself, take a moment to remember that prayer is not always easy, nor does it always focus on things that are easily understood or lived!

Read 9:21-27: In your second reading reflect on verses 23-25 until you feel you have greater insight into their meaning.

Reflection: In our culture, phrases like "losing one's life" or "saving one's life" carry strong connotations having to do with our physical life or death. Give yourself permission to let go of such understandings in order to hear these phrases in another light. When Jesus speaks of saving one's life, he is probably referring to the way we cling to what our culture teaches us to value . . . material things, reputation, a secure future, etc. When he speaks of losing one's life, he means giving up such things in order to be in touch with the more important values of God's reign. It might be helpful to reflect on 1 Corinthians 1:21-25.

Prayer: Ask for the grace to understand that "God's foolishness is wiser than human wisdom, and what seems to be God's weakness is stronger than human strength" (1 Cor. 1:25).

Rousing themselves, they saw his glory

Commentary: The synoptic Gospels all tell of John the Baptist's preaching in the desert followed immediately by the baptism of Jesus, which serves to confirm John's prediction about "the one who is to come." In each account, the Spirit appears in the form of a dove, accompanied by a voice from heaven saying, "You are my own dear son. I am pleased with you." The Transfiguration follows the same pattern after Jesus' prediction of the passion. Moses and Elijah appear, representing the Law and the Prophets, followed by the confirming voice from heaven (this time addressed to the three disciples) saying, "This is my Son, whom I have chosen—listen to him!" (Luke adds, "while he was praying" to both stories.) This is the final manifestation of Jesus' identity as the Son of God and suffering servant. The model for the Transfiguration is likely the story of Moses, who experienced God on Mount Sinai and then appeared to the people with a shining face (Exod. 24:12-18 and 34:29-35).

Preparation: Have you watched the smoke and sparks of a crackling campfire rise higher and higher until they disappeared into the night sky? Recall such a time and allow the distractions of your day to disappear like the sparks from a fire.

Read 9:28-36: In your second reading of these verses try to put yourself in the place of Peter, James, or John.

Reflection: While there have been many attempts to explain the Transfiguration in rational terms, it may be best to let it remain a mystery. Whatever happened to change the appearance of Jesus' face clearly changed Peter, James, and John as well. They "saw Jesus' glory," heard the voice from the cloud, and finally understood what kind of Messiah he was. It may be that "glory" is to God what style is to Bach or Rembrandt. Allow yourself to see, feel, and accept the glory of Jesus Christ, the servant of God.

Prayer: Pray that you may accept God's glory as a mystery to be appreciated, rather than a puzzle to be solved.

I begged your disciples to drive it out, but they couldn't.

Commentary: Our curiosity was aroused in 9:10 when Luke said, "the apostles came back and told Jesus everything they had done." Whatever the content of their report may have been, they seem uncertain about themselves in the succeeding events: the feeding of the multitude, Jesus' prediction of his suffering and death, and the Transfiguration. Now, in verses 37-50, Luke offers us four vignettes which portray the disciples as ineffective and in need of further instruction. In the first it is their inability to heal a boy suffering from epilepsy. The story implies that they had the power to heal and that their power was known to others. But at least in this instance they were unable to do so. Did they lose confidence in themselves? Were they or others lacking in faith? Or were they caught off balance by what Jesus said to them about his coming suffering and death?

Preparation: As you pray these verses, try to remember a time when someone counted on you for help and you found yourself unable to do what was needed.

Read 9:37-43a: Imagine the scene in your mind: Jesus, Peter, John, and James have just come down the mountain and encountered the crowd. Now go back and read it again, trying to be in touch with the *feelings* of all those in the story.

Reflection: With whom did you most strongly empathize in this story? Why? What do you think of Jesus' impatience in verse 41? How do you think the disciples felt when they heard him speak this way? If you have ever been asked to help someone who had confidence in you, only to discover that you couldn't do what was requested, what do you think it was that kept you from being able to help?

Prayer: Let your prayer focus on your own feelings after your reflection on this story.

They could not understand it, and they were afraid to ask

Commentary: In a second vignette Luke again addresses the quandary of the disciples. We have just heard that "all the people were amazed at the mighty power of God" demonstrated by Jesus' healing the boy with epilepsy. Peter, James, and John have just witnessed the power of God directly in the Transfiguration experience. Yet Jesus repeats the prediction about his own death saying, I am "going to be handed over to the power of men"! For the disciples the question remained . . . what kind of Messiah is it who possesses the power of God, yet is still subject to the power of mere human beings?

Preparation: We, like the disciples find such things difficult to understand. Is this not all the more reason to put aside lesser worries for the moment and give ourselves fully to listening to what the scripture is trying to tell us?

Read 9:43b-45: Read these phrases slowly and reflectively as if you were one of the disciples struggling to understand this seeming contradiction of the meaning of power.

Reflection: Can you imagine the frustration of the disciples as they struggled to understand? With their own eyes, they have seen the unbelievable power and authority of Jesus and even shared some of it! But now he tells them that he does not have (or refuses to exercise) power over his own destiny. Don't most of us share the disciples' questions, even though we have the advantage of knowing what happened in Jerusalem? Even though we have heard again and again the theological explanations about the power of redemptive suffering? Reflect for a moment on the words, "they could not understand it, and they were afraid to ask." Have you had experiences in your own life when you couldn't understand something, yet were afraid to ask?

Prayer: Give yourself permission to ask God things you have not understood, and have been afraid to ask.

[117]

LUKE 9:46-48 (NRSV)

The least among all of you is the greatest

Commentary: How long can any group of people live or work together without making comparisons about their respective personalities, contributions, or talents? We can only speculate about the causes of the argument that broke out among the disciples. In this third vignette Luke doesn't give us any details. This soon after the Transfiguration, perhaps there was jealousy about the special privilege of Peter, James, and John. Perhaps they were comparing notes about their respective successes when Jesus sent them out on their own; perhaps they were blaming one another for their failure to heal the boy with epilepsy. Whatever it was they lost any sense of humility. Jesus, recognizing the nature of the argument, placed a child before them. In the culture of the time, children did not enjoy the esteem that we would like to think they do in our own time. A child was thought of in almost the same category as a servant. Thus, to show special hospitality to a child was to humble oneself. And in the upside-down values of God's reign, "the least is the greatest."

Preparation: Consciously set aside any thought of your own greatness. "Blessed are those who are humble."

Read 9:46-48: Read the version of this teaching in Mark 9:33-37. Then, after a brief pause, read it in Luke.

Reflection: Can you remember a time when you were involved in an argument about greatness, importance, ability, or some other human quality? What was concluded? How did you feel about the discussion? How did you feel about yourself? Imagine Jesus overhearing that discussion and calling into your presence a homeless person off the street, saying to you, "Whoever welcomes this homeless person in my name, welcomes me. . . ." What are the limits of hospitality in your life?

Prayer: Give thanks for the hospitality that has been extended to you by God and by other persons in your life. Ask for the humility to offer such hospitality to anyone who needs it.

[118]

He doesn't belong to our group

Commentary: The fourth of Luke's glimpses brings to a close the Galilean ministry of Jesus. In it we encounter the struggle of the disciples with the self-righteousness that sometimes characterizes those who see themselves as part of an exclusive group. They have fallen into the trap of thinking that because they are "close to Jesus" they are somehow better than others who act out of similar values. It is a childish attitude that many, if not all, of us have been guilty of at one time or another.

Preparation: Before you read and reflect on these two verses, take a moment to get in touch with a similar attitude that you or someone you know has about your church, your family, or your social grouping. Then prepare yourself for prayer as usual.

Read 9:49-50: After reading these verses once, go back and read them again slowly as if you were there witnessing the original incident. Listen for the inflection in John's voice as he speaks about someone else using Jesus' name.

Reflection: Do you know people who brag about going to heaven because of their closeness to Jesus? Because they go to church every week? Because they keep the Ten Commandments? Do you know people who look down their noses at others who don't go to church? What about the person who is a little too proud of being a charter member of the church? What about those in the body of Christ who believe that they and those who believe as they do are true Christians while others are not real Christians? Perhaps we all need to remember that when someone is thirsty, it doesn't make any difference whose idea it is to give him or her a drink of water. Nor does it make any difference who holds the cup, or whose name is on the cup. The only thing that matters is that the person is given a drink of water.

Prayer: Ask God's forgiveness for the attitude we sometimes have that causes us to exclude others who "don't belong to our group."

THE JOURNEY TO JERUSALEM
LUKE 9:51–19:27

When the days drew near for him to be taken up,
he set his face to go to Jerusalem.
(Luke 9:51, NRSV)

IN HIS ACCOUNT OF THE TRANSFIGURATION, Luke begins to turn the reader's attention from Galilee to Jerusalem. Unlike Matthew and Mark, he has Moses and Elijah, "[talking] with Jesus about the way he would soon fulfill God's purpose by dying in Jerusalem." Then, at 9:51, Jesus' ministry in Galilee comes to an abrupt end as Luke says, "As the days drew near for him to be taken up, he set his face to go to Jerusalem."

Thus begins the second major block of material having to do with Jesus' ministry. One of the most distinguishing characteristics of this section is its journey motif, of which there are repeated reminders throughout the narrative (9:51,53; 13:22,33; 17:11; 18:31; 19:11; and 19:28). Those who think of "journey" as a consistent geographical movement toward Jerusalem will be disappointed. The movement is theological and editorial rather than geographical. The only real geographical focus is Jerusalem itself.

If Luke had an overall plan or structure for his journey narrative it has eluded scholars. A. E. Harvey's suggestion, admittedly speculative, may well be accurate:

> We must imagine that Luke had received a substantial amount of information about Jesus' teaching and activities which had no fixed place in any connected narrative, and which he had to work in as best he could. He knew that, at a certain point, Jesus travelled from Galilee to Jerusalem; and it occurred to him to fill out the picture of Jesus as a travelling teacher . . . by inserting into this journey most of the extra material which he possessed.[40]

Harvey's suggestion is supported by the fact that only a very small amount of the material in the journey narrative came from Mark while a substantial portion of it comes from Luke's independent sources. Two themes are prominent throughout the narrative: "Jesus goes to his death" and "Jesus instructs his disciples."

He made up his mind and set out
on his way to Jerusalem

Commentary: The ministry in Galilee is completed. With the statement that Jesus "made up his mind and set out on his way to Jerusalem," Luke begins another major section of his Gospel. The NRSV is even stronger: "he set his face to go to Jerusalem." Luke probably had in mind the words from Isaiah's servant song, "therefore I have set my face like flint, and I know that I shall not be put to shame" (Isaiah 50:7b, NRSV). With few exceptions the material in 9:51–19:28 is either unique to Luke or derives from the source common to Luke and Matthew. As his ministry in Galilee began with rejection in the synagogue at Nazareth, the journey to Jerusalem begins with rejection by a village in Samaria. This incident provides us yet another example of the disciples' inability to live up to the standards set out by Jesus. Not content to "shake the dust off their sandals" as a warning to the hostile villagers, James and John call for revenge and are thus rebuked by Jesus.

Preparation: Recall a time when you decided to "set your face" toward a difficult task and get on with it.

Read 9:51-56: In your first reading try to view this event through the eyes of the disciples; then read it again as you feel Jesus himself may have experienced it.

Reflection: Jesus has already spoken twice to his disciples about his coming suffering and death. Peter, James, and John have been instructed by the voice from the cloud on the mountain to "listen to him." Now, the prediction begins to move toward reality as Jesus begins the difficult journey to Jerusalem. Imagine for a few moments that you are among the disciples with him as the journey starts. What do you feel? How much do you understand? How do you react when the people of the Samaritan village will not receive him? How do you feel about Jesus' rebuke?

Prayer: Begin with your feelings. Ask for greater understanding of "the suffering servant."

I will follow you . . . but first . . .

Commentary: When Jesus first spoke to his disciples about his own suffering, death, and resurrection, he challenged them to take up their crosses and follow him. Now, having set his face toward Jerusalem, he again challenges those who would follow him to consider the cost of discipleship. When the first person says, "I will follow you wherever you go," Jesus' answer is a reminder that to do so is to abandon the security of home and to depend upon others for hospitality. He answers the second and third persons by telling them that following him is more important than family relationships and responsibilities. Those who follow him must "set their faces" as firmly on the way of suffering as Jesus himself has done. For more insight into the illustration about plowing and looking back, see 1 Kings 19:19-21.

Preparation: Can you remember a time when you were challenged to do something so important that it meant choosing against your own family or other personal priorities?

Read 9:57-62: After reading these verses once, go back to read them again, pausing to reflect briefly on the words of the three anonymous persons.

Reflection: This glimpse into the responses of three would-be followers of Jesus is an attempt to convict us concerning the radical nature of discipleship. It is not like joining a service club or volunteering to help with a charity drive. It involves a willingness to let go of the things of the world in order to give one's self to the things of the reign of God. Christians in every age have looked for ways to compromise the radical nature of this call. How have you heard the call to follow Christ? What has your response been? What compromises do you seek of its radical nature? How do you rationalize your own style of discipleship? What challenge do you hear in this passage for you personally?

Prayer: Pray for the courage to answer the call as you have experienced it.

I am sending you like lambs among wolves

Commentary: A tradition of the rabbis, based on the Septuagint version of Genesis 10, says that there were seventy-two nations in the world. Thus the mission of the seventy-two, found only in this Gospel, may be Luke's way of emphasizing the importance of taking the gospel to the whole world. The urgency of the mission is stressed both by the need to pray for more workers and by the instruction not to waste time to greet anyone on the road. The missionaries are sent out in pairs and are instructed to stay in the homes where they are first welcomed rather than looking around for better accommodations! Notice that the same message, "the Kingdom of God has come near you," is to be given both to those who accept and to those who reject the missionary effort of the disciples.

Preparation: As you quiet your spirit and let go of the day's agenda, give yourself permission to carry with you at the end of your time of prayer the peace you feel in these moments. Pause as needed during the day to take a deep breath and recall it.

Read 10:1-12: In your second reading, think of yourself as one of the seventy-two being sent out to witness to the Kingdom of God.

Reflection: Being faithful to the gospel means being sent out to witness every day, an opportunity we don't always relish! Take time to reflect on the instructions Jesus gave the seventy-two and see what you might learn about your own witness. What does it mean to be sent "like lambs among wolves"? How do you feel about not stopping to greet anyone on the road? How do you feel about accepting the hospitality offered to you by those you encounter in life? When is it appropriate for you to wipe off the dust of a place where you are not welcomed? How do people know after being in relationship with you that "the Kingdom of God has come near" them?

Prayer: Pray for the effectiveness of your own witness wherever it is that you are in mission.

Whoever listens to you listens to me

Commentary: The material in verses 12-15 comes from the source common to both Matthew and Luke. Matthew's introduction sets it in perspective:

> The people in the towns where Jesus had performed most of his miracles did not turn from their sins, so he reproached those towns.   (Matthew 11:20, TEV)

Luke uses it to reinforce what he has said to the seventy-two about towns where they are not welcomed. Chorazin may have been a town just northeast of Capernaum. According to Jesus' judgment, even the Gentile cities of Tyre and Sidon would have responded more favorably had he performed his miracles in them. The strength of his condemnation of Capernaum is somewhat surprising since Jesus had spent a considerable amount of time there and even made it his headquarters in Galilee. The charge to the seventy-two concludes with verse 16, which emphasizes the authority of the disciples.

Preparation: Sometimes a portion of scripture almost seems to pray itself in us when we read it. At other times we find ourselves struggling, either because the passage is difficult or because we are not prepared to hear it. The important thing is to be faithful to the process. Such readings may surprise us.

Read 10:13-16: First read the parallel passage in Matthew 11:20-24. Then come back to Luke, beginning with 10:10 and continuing through verse 16.

Reflection: Imagine hearing these words as one of those being commissioned by Jesus. What emotions do you hear in Jesus' voice? What questions do you have as you hear judgment pronounced on Chorazin, Bethsaida, and Capernaum? What do you think Jesus would say about the city where you live? How do you feel about the authority given to the disciples in verse 16?

Prayer: Let your prayer begin with your reflections.

[125]

I have given you authority, . . . and nothing will hurt you

Commentary: The enthusiasm of the returning disciples and Jesus' response to it are expressed in language subject to interpretation. How much of it reflects the events of Jesus' time and how much the time of Luke's writing? In speaking of "the power of the enemy" that Jesus has enabled his followers to overcome, Luke may also be thinking about the persecution of the early church. Was Jesus proclaiming the beginning of the "new age" when he spoke of Satan falling from heaven, or is this part of his warning (verse 20) that those who returned should not glory in their own successes? The prize, as Jerome Kodell says, "is not human glory through feats of power but heavenly glory through following Jesus to Jerusalem, to Calvary."[41]

Preparation: When you are prepared to read and pray these verses, pause to ask yourself if *all* of you is ready . . . your spirit and your body, as well as your mind.

Read 10:17-20: Before your second reading, you may want to return to the introduction to see if there are any questions or suggestions there that will be helpful to you.

Reflection: In the midst of our daily routines some occasions stand out as special. Sometimes things really "click," and we feel a sudden sense of accomplishment. "I really did that very well," we say as we rejoice in a special accomplishment. On the other hand, Jesus seems to be saying that in such times we may be vulnerable to being *too* proud. These may be the times to ask ourselves, did *I* do it? Or did God enable it to happen through me? What is it that makes it possible for such things to happen through us? Is it not through our *giving up* our pride and allowing ourselves to become servants that we receive the authority to overcome "the power of the enemy"?

Prayer: Ask God to remind you that it is only by your willingness to be a servant that you are given such authority.

You hid all this from . . . educated people and showed it to ordinary people

Commentary: Some have called Luke 10:1-24 a service of sending the disciples and then receiving them back from their mission. If so, verses 21-24 constitute a prayer of thanksgiving for their success and a final blessing on those who have seen what the wise and educated have failed to see. Matthew uses the same material in different contexts, one after Jesus' condemnation of Chorazin and Capernaum for not responding to his ministry (Matt. 11:25-27), and the other as a compliment to the disciples as he explains the purpose of his parables (Matt. 13:16-17). The point in each case is that God's upside-down wisdom is understood best by those we might least expect to understand. Notice the footnote to verse 21 in most good translations, pointing out that the early manuscripts differ as to whether the phrase in 10:21 should be translated "by the Holy Spirit," by "the Spirit," or "in his spirit."

Preparation: Take a moment to reflect on these words from Isaiah: " 'My thoughts,' says the Lord, 'are not like yours, and my ways are different from yours' " (Isaiah 55:8, TEV).

Read 10:21-24: Read the passage twice as usual, allowing it to speak to you.

Reflection: Have there been times when you didn't understand something because you were trying to make it too complicated? Verse 21 refers to God's hiding such knowledge from wise or educated people. Do you think the problem is that God hides understanding from us, or are we unprepared to understand? How do you think you might allow yourself to be more open to understanding such things?

Prayer: Ask God to help you do away with those things, attitudes, and beliefs that get in the way of your understanding what others can more readily understand.

LUKE 10:25-37 (TEV)

Which one of these three acted like a neighbor?

Commentary: Luke's telling of this story is much more creative than either Matthew or Mark. Here Jesus encourages the teacher of the Law to answer his own question and then moves the conversation beyond the quotations from the Shema (Deut. 6:4-5) and the loving of one's neighbor (Lev. 19:18). It isn't just a matter of *knowing*, Jesus says, but of *doing*. Like any good lawyer, the teacher asks another question, "Who is my neighbor?" By telling a story Jesus again allows the teacher to answer his own question. The story invited him to think beyond the mere observance of the Law, which provided plenty of excuses for the priest and the Levite to avoid caring for the man beside the road. It also invites him (and us) to think before prejudging others. The reading ends with a second reminder that the Law is to be observed, not just by *knowing*, but *doing* it.

Preparation: Pray this story honestly by calling to mind a person or group that you tend to avoid or feel superior to.

Read 10:25-37: Read the story. Take a moment to imagine both Jesus' conversation with the teacher of the Law and the scene involving the man on the road to Jericho. Then go back and read the story again.

Reflection: Who is that person that you avoid or feel superior to? What does that person or group need? Imagine a situation where such a need is expressed by that person. What excuses, however legitimate, come to mind for your not responding? If you don't overcome your reasons for not helping, who will help, and under what conditions? Have you ever been assisted by someone you would never have expected to offer you help? If so, how did you feel? What risks might you be willing to take in the future to help someone in need?

Prayer: Pray for your own need to hear what God wants you to do and for the courage to do it. Pray for the person or persons that you would be reluctant to help.

[128]

Mary has chosen the right thing

Commentary: The teacher in the preceding story was so busy *studying* the Law he didn't know how to *follow* it. Now Martha is so busy doing, that she doesn't have time to listen to the Messiah in her own living room! Notice that Jesus chastises neither for his or her choice, but merely reminds them of the need for balance. But there is much more here. When Luke tells us that Mary "sat down at the feet of the Lord," he is telling us that she was treated as a disciple . . . a radical departure from the traditions of the time that precluded a rabbi from even speaking to a woman. The same point is made even more strongly in John 4:1-42.

Preparation: Recall examples from your own experience of the continuing debate in the church between those who stress "personal salvation" and those who stress "social action."

Read 10:38-42: Hear the story first through the ears of Martha, slaving away in the kitchen. Then hear it again with Mary, who hangs on to Jesus' every word.

Reflection: Consider this wonderful story from the Desert Fathers and Mothers of the fourth century:

> A certain brother came to Abbot Silvanus at Mount Sinai, and seeing the hermits at work he exclaimed: Why do you work for the bread that perisheth? Mary has chosen the best part, namely to sit at the feet of the Lord without working. Then the Abbot gave the brother a book and an empty cell in which to read it. After a while the brother got hungry and went to find the Abbot to inquire about dinner. Informed that the others had already eaten, the brother asked, "Why did you not call me?" "You are a spiritual man," the Abbot replied, "you do not need the food that perishes. We have to work, but you have chosen the better part." Hearing this the brother asked to be forgiven. It was because Martha worked that Mary was able to be praised.[42]

Prayer: Pray to be shown every day the need for a balance between hearing the word and doing it.

[129]

Lord, teach us to pray

Commentary: The following compilation showing *some* of the differences between the Matthew and Luke versions of the Lord's Prayer illustrates that the prayer as we know it today is probably quite different than the prayer the disciples may have learned from Jesus. The words in italics represent some of Matthew's additions and interpretations as distinguished from Luke's shorter version. Other differences, beyond the scope of this brief commentary, may reflect subtle theological and cultural assumptions of the Luke and Matthew communities.

> *Our* Father *in heaven,*
> May your holy name be honored;
> may your Kingdom come.
> *May your will be done on earth as it is in heaven.*
> Give us day by day *(today)* the food we need.
> Forgive us our sins,
> for we forgive everyone who does us wrong.
> And do not bring us to hard testing.
> *But keep us safe from the Evil One.*

Preparation: Let your preparation, reflection, and prayer all begin with, "Lord, teach us to pray."

Read: 11:1-4: Read Matthew's version first. Then read the prayer as it is in Luke's Gospel.

Reflection: That the church through the ages has followed Matthew's version of the Lord's Prayer can be seen in the fact that the King James Version included most of the Matthean additions, even though they were *not* part of the original manuscripts! It even appended the doxological ending, "for thine is the kingdom, and the power, and the glory, for ever. Amen," which had by that time become common liturgical practice. Set aside some time to read both versions of the prayer in several different translations.

Prayer: Using your own favorite translation, allow the saints of many centuries to pray this great prayer with you.

Ask . . . seek . . . knock

Commentary: Unlike Matthew, Luke extends the giving of the Lord's Prayer to include a parable and three sayings that focus on the need for persistence in prayer. Their purpose, however, is to remind us that God's desire to respond to our need is even greater than our own willingness to answer the need of friends or even family members. Matthew does not include the parable of the friend at midnight, but does use the "Ask, seek, and knock" sayings in a different context. In these, two differences are worth noting. When Luke asks what father would give his son a scorpion when he asks for an egg, Matthew has a stone for bread. Of greater significance is the final sentence in which Matthew says God will "give good things" to those who ask, and Luke says God will "give the Holy Spirit" to those who ask.

Preparation: Do you persist in asking for what you need or are you more likely to alter your request when a response is slow in coming?

Read 11:5-13: With the idea of persistence in prayer in mind, read verses 5-8; pause, then read them again. Do the same things for the sayings in verses 9-13. Then read the whole section together.

Reflection: The parable in verses 5-8 is a bit awkward because of its focus on the response of the neighbor rather than the persistence of the person who needs to borrow bread. Still the point is well made. Can you remember a time when something like that happened to you and you were "not ashamed to keep on asking" because your need was so great? Have you ever been on the other end with someone persistently seeking your help? If we are willing to respond in such a situation, how much more is God not only willing, but anxious to give us the gift of the Holy Spirit? Dare we stop asking, even when we are discouraged or ashamed?

Prayer: Ask God, who is more than willing to give the gift of the Spirit, to help you to be persistent in prayer . . . and open to the answers that come.

Anyone who is not for me is really against me

Commentary: Having told us that God is not only willing but anxious to give the Holy Spirit to those who seek it, Luke now reminds us that we often resist God's gifts even when they are made obvious. This message comes in the reactions of those who witnessed Jesus' exorcism of a demon that prevented a man from talking. The amazement of the crowds leaves no doubt about the fact of the exorcism. The question they asked Jesus was not, "did you do it?" but "how did you do it?" Some asserted that Jesus must have been acting on behalf of Beelzebul, the prince of demons. Others asked for another miracle to prove that his power came from God. Jesus responded with logic—why would the prince of demons destroy one of his own? No, it is by the stronger power of God, illustrated by the mini-parable in 21-22 that Jesus used. Luke concludes with a saying that challenges the cynicism and unbelief of the questioners, "Anyone who is not for me is really against me."

Preparation: Begin your preparation with a prayer for openness to receive whatever God offers you in this experience.

Read 11:14-23: First, note the details of this scene: the exorcism, the crowd's reaction, Jesus' response, and the concluding saying. Then read it again imagining it from Jesus' point of view.

Reflection: Can you recall a time when you did something good, only to have others question your motivation? What about a time when you questioned someone else's motivation rather than accepting the kindness as a gift? How does this relate to the statement, "Anyone who is not for me is really against me; anyone who does not help me gather is really scattering"? Is this like our saying, "if you can't say anything good, don't say anything at all"?

Prayer: Ask God to help you accept and celebrate the grace that comes through the words and deeds of others, rather than questioning their motives.

It . . . brings seven other spirits more evil than itself

Commentary: The image of the house in verse 21 is now followed with the parable that calls the human body a house where unclean spirits (demons) dwell. When a demon is cast out it "wanders through waterless regions looking for a resting place." Such "disembodied spirits" were believed to inhabit wilderness areas. Finding no resting place, the demon returns to its house, the person from whom it had been exorcised. The parable is meant as a warning to those from whom such unclean spirits have been exorcised. They need to put their house in order and fill it with good to avoid the return of the old problems or new ones that may be even worse.

Preparation: As you center yourself, be aware that in so doing you are inviting "good spirits" into your "house," whose presence will make it all the more difficult for you to entertain "evil spirits."

Read 11:24-26: Read these three verses in light of the introduction above. Then go back and look at verses 21 and 22.

Reflection: Who among us does not know the difficulty of eliminating from our lives some sin or bad habit? Bad habits don't die easily! How long do we live with it, knowing that it should be cast out of our life? How many times do we resolve to be done with it . . . tomorrow. How easy it is for us to rationalize that the problem is really not so bad; after all, it could be worse! Then we finally take the first step to change. What follows is the critical time. We have cleaned our house, which may only serve to make the habit more attractive. And how easy it is for the habit to "move back in" on us. Luke seems to be saying that the need is not only to cast out the evil in us, but to put something good in its place, so that there will no longer be room for it to return.

Prayer: Pray for new insight into the part of yourself that wants to cast out the evil in you, yet often welcomes it back.

How happy is the woman who bore you

Commentary: The praise of Jesus' mother offers a specific example to illustrate Luke's earlier statement (verse 14) that there were some in the crowd who approved of what he did. Jesus' response is the same response he made when his mother and brothers appeared earlier (8:19). The fact that it is repeated here may reflect Luke's general following of the Markan order, since Mark places the story of Jesus' mother and brothers after the account of Jesus and Beelzebul. In any case it seems to suggest that the way to keep an exorcised spirit from returning is to "hear the word of God and obey it."

Preparation: As you prepare again to pray the words of Luke's Gospel, ask yourself if you are among those who are happy to hear the word of God and obey it.

Read 11:27-28: Before you read this passage, go back and look again at the context in which it is found, beginning with verse 14. Note the other reactions that are in sharp contrast to that of the woman in verse 27.

Reflection: The anonymous woman is obviously an admirer of Jesus. Perhaps she identifies with his mother when she says, "Happy is the woman who bore you. . . ." How do you think this woman felt when she heard Jesus respond, "Rather, how happy are those who hear the word of God and obey it"? Did she feel put down for her suggestion? Or did she take it as a further demonstration of Jesus' wisdom? Is Jesus saying that his relationship with his mother is not important, or is he reminding her that what is really important is keeping our eyes focused on the reign of God?

Prayer: Ask God to help you understand the meaning of this brief dialogue in the midst of the crowd.

There is something here greater than Jonah!

Commentary: With different examples Luke now repeats the message to those in the synagogue at Nazareth (4:25-27) that foreigners may be more responsive to Jesus' message than the people of Israel. Jesus is a sign for them to an even greater extent than Jonah was a sign to the people of Nineveh who responded with repentance. Even the Queen of Sheba serves as a judgment on the people of Israel because of her listening to King Solomon. Jesus' opening remark about "evil" people is a response to those in the crowd who made the request for a miracle (verse 16). At the same time it may be an extension of the thought in verse 26, that simply being healed of an evil spirit is not enough. One must also be open to the word. Those who are not are subject to doubt, among other things.

Preparation: Before praying this section, can you get in touch with some of your own reluctance to follow Jesus?

Read 11:29-32: Recall the story of Jonah and the response of the people of Nineveh to his preaching. Now read these verses and remember the response of the people in this crowd.

Reflection: How we like to have our authorities "certified"! We don't want just any lawyer, nurse, or plumber. We want to know that he or she is qualified and has a proven track record. Luke has already told us that the people "were all amazed at the way he taught, because he spoke with authority" (4:32). Such reactions are repeated several times in the Gospels. Yet such "authority" or charisma is not enough for our rational western minds . . . or even the minds of many of our spiritual ancestors in the Middle East. We want proof. And even repeated miracles are seldom enough to convince us.

Prayer: Pray again for God to show you the difference between knowledge and faith.

[135]

Be sure that your light is not darkness

Commentary: Luke returns to the saying about lighting a lamp, already used in 8:16, but this time he extends it in such a way that the human body becomes a simile also. "Your eyes are like a lamp." It seems to be an additional response to those who seek proof of Jesus' authority through another miracle. God's word is enough. It brings light to us if we accept it and allow it to fill our being, so that it may then been seen in us by others.

Preparation: If you are praying this scripture at night and have a kerosene lantern or a candle available, light it and use it as you continue to read and pray.

Read 11:33-36: As you read these verses the first time, concentrate on the image of a lamp and the light it gives, making it possible for us to see in the darkness. Then read it again and reflect on the light in you that can help others to "see in the darkness."

Reflection: What do you think of the statement that, "your eyes are like a lamp for the body"? Think about the eyes of people you know. Sometimes we speak of a person's eyes as "shining," "dull," "brilliant," "sparkling," etc. Can you think of other expressions that refer to the light of a person's eyes? We also speak of a person's mood or state of health as showing in his or her eyes. Think about eyes that show excitement, joy, depression, sadness, love, anger, longing. Do our eyes not show to others something about who we are in relation to God? And do they not convey our spiritual health as well as our physical health? What do others see when they look into your eyes? What can you do to let the light shine in your eyes?

Prayer: Pray that your body might be "full of light" and that others may be able to see the light of the gospel in your eyes.

How terrible for you Pharisees!

Commentary: Those who think about "gentle Jesus, meek and mild" should look again at this passage! Luke sets it in the home of a Pharisee where Jesus is an invited guest. When the host asks why Jesus has not washed before eating, Jesus offers three major criticisms of the Pharisees: they emphasize external observances of the Law while neglecting justice and love; they seek honor and acclaim for themselves; and they are like unmarked graves, contaminating others because of their hypocrisy (Matthew's parallel (23:1-36) has this episode near the Temple, perhaps on the southern steps, where the "whitewashed tombs" on the Mount of Olives could easily be seen). Then, in 45-52, Jesus lashes out at the teachers of the Law, accusing them of avoiding the legal burdens they place on others; assenting to the murder of the prophets while pretending to honor them; and of not practicing what they preach. Not surprisingly, the episode ends with the Pharisees and teachers of the Law looking for a way to discredit Jesus.

Preparation: Be prepared to hear an angry Jesus say things we are not accustomed to hearing in polite table conversation!

Read 11:37-54: You might find it helpful to read Matthew's version first (23:1-36), and then come back to Luke for your second reading. Take time to imagine the scene in both cases.

Reflection: Jesus' relationship with the Pharisees is interesting. Although they tested each other in public debates and seemed to be at odds with each other, Jesus was probably closer to the Pharisees than to any other group in Israel. They held many views in commmon, and often conversed, ate, and worshiped together. How did you *feel* as you listened in on this dinner conversation? How do you think Jesus' host felt? Knowing that there is something of the Pharisee in most of us, how do you think Jesus might address you over dinner in your home?

Prayer: Ask God to help you to see the Pharisee inside you and to hear Jesus speaking to your hypocrisy.

Whatever you have whispered in private . . . will be shouted from the housetops

Commentary: The crowd now numbers in the thousands and people press in on every side. Jesus, having just spoken about the hypocrisy of the Pharisees and lawyers, now warns his disciples about their own hypocrisy. This "private" conversation itself becomes an illustration of his point, because others in the crowd could easily listen in. Luke is not simply reporting traditional teachings of Jesus, but is putting them together in ways that address the situations he knows all too well in the early church. The warnings about hypocrisy are thus aimed, not just at the disciples, but at those in Luke's church and our own! Fred Craddock suggests that these words may point to a kind of reverse hypocrisy in which people pretend *not* to be followers of Jesus when they actually are.[43] Peter's denial on the night of Jesus' arrest is only one example. There were others like Nicodemus, who perhaps had good reason to be secretive, at least for a time. Both kinds of hypocrisy will be made known in the ultimate scheme of things.

Preparation: Be aware that the words in these verses are addressed to your hypocrisy as well as that of those who may have heard the message from the lips of Jesus.

Read 12:1-3: As you read, remember Jesus' harsh words to the Pharisees and teachers of the Law in the previous passage.

Reflection: Has anyone among us not been accused of hypocrisy? We have all nodded yes to conversational points with which we really disagreed. We have all pretended to be one thing when in reality we were something else. This includes, as Craddock points out, pretending not to be something that we really are. The sayings in these verses are a sobering reminder that "whatever we whisper in private . . . will be shouted from the housetops."

Prayer: Begin your prayer with an honest confession of your own hypocrisy and continue according to your own needs.

I will show you whom to fear

Commentary: Luke's recurring theme, "do not be afraid," appears twice in these four verses. Against the backdrop of the persecution suffered by those in the early church, the message is clear. The power of God's judgment upon hypocritical disciples is more to be feared than the possibility of death as a result of persecution. One thinks of Martin Luther's hymn:

> Let goods and kindred go,
> this mortal life also;
> the body they may kill;
> God's truth abideth still;
> his kingdom is forever.[44]

The fear of persecution is not the real issue. The God who knows us in every detail, and even cares about sparrows, will certainly care for Jesus' disciples! And speaking of sparrows, Luke seems to have had an eye for a bargain. While the sparrows in Matthew sell two for a penny, Luke's price is five for two pennies!

Preparation: As you read and pray, try to remember a time when you felt afraid because of some circumstance in your life.

Read 12:4-7: Focus first on the fear expressed in verses 4-5, and then God's care expounded on in verses 6-7.

Reflection: Most of us live out our lives in times and places where not much is expected of us as we witness to our faith. However, there were many in the early church whose Christian faith cost them their lives! In such a time martyrdom came to be seen as a badge of honor. Thus the statement that we should not be afraid of those who can only take our lives, but do nothing to us afterward. What in your faith is so important to you that you would be willing to give up your life for it? How could your witness be more meaningful, short of martyrdom?

Prayer: Allow God to listen in as you reflect on these questions. Ask God to show you how important your faith really is.

The Holy Spirit will teach you . . . what you ought to say

Commentary: Verses 8-12 continue the discussion of Christian witness in a time of persecution. The focus now is on one's understanding of the Holy Spirit. One can be forgiven, Luke says, for speaking against Jesus out of ignorance. But to speak against the Holy Spirit is to speak against the very source of one's own relationship with God and is thus unforgivable. To speak in this way is to curse the very power that works in us as we witness to our faith.

Preparation: Remember a time when you were called upon to offer some witness to your faith and felt inadequate to do so.

Read 12:8-12: Read this teaching twice, pausing between readings for a moment or two of quiet. Listen for the words that address you today.

Reflection: There was a time in our recent history when most Christians shared a similar understanding of what it meant to "witness to Christ." But today this phrase often means different things to different people. For some it calls forth a need for public affirmation of certain classic doctrines. For others, witnessing evokes a much more personal response. And there are still others for whom the idea of "witnessing to Christ" stirs feelings ranging from embarrassment to fear. How do you respond to the idea of "witnessing to Christ"? What kind of witness would you be comfortable making? How do you feel about Luke's statement that, "the Holy Spirit will teach you at that time what you should say"? What would it take for you to be more open to the leading of the Spirit of God in your life and in your witness?

Prayer: Ask God to listen to you as you reflect on these questions. Ask for the guidance of the Spirit in your life and for the courage to be a witness to Christ.

One's life does not consist in the abundance of possessions

Commentary: Luke's special concern about money and possessions was first raised in Mary's song (1:53). We hear it now in an incident and a parable not found in either Matthew or Mark. In a request reminiscent of Martha in 10:40, Jesus is asked to settle a family dispute, this time having to do with the division of an inheritance between two brothers. The man asking the question was quite likely the younger brother who, according to the Law, would have been entitled only to a smaller share of the property. Refusing to answer the question directly, Jesus instead addresses the spiritual issue that lies beneath it, both with the observation in verse 15 and the parable that follows.

Preparation: Place your checkbook or credit cards in front of you before you begin to pray this scripture reading.

Read 12:13-21: Imagine the scene in verses 13-15. Then read the entire section through the end of the parable.

Reflection: Leo Tolstoy told a story about a farmer who was promised that he could have all the land he could walk around between sunrise and sunset on a single day. The man started off at the crack of dawn. He saw a fertile field and he wanted it; then he saw a beautiful woods and he wanted that; and then a lake, and another field, and so on. Soon he was running, trying to get around every attractive piece of land he saw. Late in the afternoon, he realized that he was far from home and had to make it back before sunset in order for all this land to be his. He began to run as fast as he could. As the sun began to set, he was exhausted and afraid he would never make it back in time. At last, just as the sun slipped beneath the horizon, he made it back to his starting point . . . where he dropped dead. All the land he needed was a plot six feet long and two feet wide.[45]

Prayer: Go back to read verse 21 again. Let your prayer begin with your response to it.

Can any of you live a bit longer by worrying about it?

Commentary: The meaning of the preceding parable is now spelled out in clear and unmistakable language. Having overcome his own temptation to turn stones into bread, Jesus challenges his followers to live by the faith that life is more than food and clothing. His injunction not to worry about such things presents a direct challenge to the lifestyle pursued by many modern Christians, especially in what might be called the world's "overdeveloped countries."

Preparation: Take a few moments to do a quick mental inventory of: 1) your closet, 2) your pantry, and 3) your insurance policies and other investments designed to "secure" your future.

Read 12:22-31: Read these verses. Pause long enough to reflect again on the "things" in your life. Then read the verses again.

Reflection: Ask yourself:
—How concerned am I about the things in my life?
—How much time, effort, and money does it take me to buy, sort, clean, insure, repair, and dispose of such things?
—How much do I worry about money, clothing, and my future material security?
—To what extent do the things in my life interfere with my seeking of the reign of God?
—How much is enough?
How do you feel about these words from Psalm 127:

> In vain do you rise early in the morning
> and go late to bed at night,
> eating the bread of anxious toil.
> For God provides for those he loves
> while they sleep.   (Psalm 127:2, AP)

Prayer: Share the fruit of your reflection with God, asking for guidance, insight, and the courage to put the reign of God before the things of this world. Your heart will always be where your riches are.

[142]

Your heart will always be where your riches are

Commentary: This section about attitudes toward money and possessions now concludes with a call for the disciples of Jesus to take a dramatic leap of faith . . . "sell all your belongings and give the money to the poor"! Appropriately, Luke introduces this challenge with the phrase he has already used several times to assure those being called to radical discipleship, "do not be afraid." Those who would trust in God are to engage in a simplicity of life that includes generous almsgiving. By thus reaching out to others, Jesus' disciples provide for themselves riches that do not perish . . . a place in the reign of God.

Preparation: Before reading and praying these three verses, pause a moment to get in touch with the feelings you have when you pay your bills. Can you let go of some of those feelings now in order to hear a different perspective on money?

Read 12:32-34: Three verses. Three very important verses. Three very challenging verses. Three verses that almost take your breath away if you have a nice savings account and a nest egg for retirement. Give these verses their due.

Reflection: Consider the words of Harry Emerson Fosdick's great hymn, "God of Grace and God of Glory."

> Cure thy children's warring madness,
> bend our pride to thy control;
> shame our wanton, selfish gladness,
> rich in things and poor in soul.
> Grant us wisdom, grant us courage,
> lest we miss thy kingdom's goal.[46]

Prayer: Ask God to help you discover what it would take to make you no longer "rich in things and poor in soul."

Be ready for whatever comes

Commentary: These two parables about the Lord's return are intended for all disciples. Later in 41-48 they will be explained in greater detail for those who are leaders. Two images: "dressed for action," and "with your lamps lit," urge us to be ready, awake, and alert. The first parable calls for servants to be ready (faithful) when the master returns from a wedding feast, even if it is very late. It is not for the servants to know exactly when the master will come, but simply to be prepared when he finally does come. Luke may have in mind the futility of the church's speculation about the date of the Lord's return. Note the reward for those who are prepared. The second parable is about a householder who is prepared for the arrival of a thief in the night, even though such an event is not anticipated.

Preparation: The parables call for preparation through faithfulness, part of which is our faithfulness in prayer.

Read 12:35-40: Read verses 35-38, pausing to imagine the scene and circumstances in your mind; continue with verse 39, reflecting briefly on the scene. Now read verse 40.

Reflection: The futility of trying to guess when the Lord will come has often been demonstrated by overzealous Christians. As verse 40 says, "the Son of Man will come at an hour when you are not expecting him." How then are we to "wait for the Lord"? Recall a time when you "waited up" late at night for someone whose time of arrival was uncertain. How did you remain ready and alert? What does it mean for us to wait for the Lord by being faithful? What do you think Isaiah meant by saying:

> *Those who wait for the Lord shall renew their strength,*
> *they shall mount up with wings like eagles,*
> *they shall run and not be weary,*
> *they shall walk and not faint.*   (Isaiah 40:31, NRSV)

Prayer: Ask God to help you to be faithful in these uncertain times of waiting and watching.

From everyone to whom much has been given, much will be required

Commentary: The parable in 35-40 is now expanded, beginning with a question raised by Peter. The question is significant because it asks whether the parable applies merely to the disciples or to everyone. How we understand *everyone* is important. Once more it is important to remember that Luke's writing comes out of the context of the early church. Thus the question really asks, was this parable relevant only to the disciples and others associated with the historical Jesus, or does it also apply to all those who followed, including Luke's readers? Jesus' answer implies that while the parable is for everyone, it is especially important for those who hold positions of leadership in the community. Those who are faithful will be blessed; those who abuse their position of trust will be punished according to their level of responsibility. This is summarized in the closing proverb.

Preparation: Before you enter into the praying of these verses, ask God to help you to be fully honest about finding their meaning for your own life.

Read 12:41-48: As you read this passage, be mindful of any responsibilities you hold in the Christian community. Read it slowly and carefully. As always, read it twice.

Reflection: Reflect on any positions of leadership with which you may have been entrusted in the Christian community or elsewhere. What kind of responsibility have you been given? What is expected of you? Who are the people who depend on you? What do they depend on you to do? In what ways might you be tempted to abuse your leadership? Where is your accountability? How do you feel about the proverb which closes this reading?

Prayer: Summarize your reflections, knowing that God has been a part of the process from the beginning. Ask God for guidance according to your needs.

I came to make people choose sides

Commentary: Luke has brought together verses 49-53, 54-56, and 57-59, even though they are widely separated in Matthew. This suggests that they were not originally part of the same context. Luke uses them well to point up the urgency of things, as Jesus moves toward his baptism (passion) experience in Jerusalem. But he has even more in mind. Again we must view these passages in the context of the experience of the early church. As LaVerdiere says, "Many must have expected that the journey would be untroubled and peaceful. However, it had become clear that fidelity to the Christian mission frequently resulted in painful conflicts and divisions even in the same family."[47] Luke thus provides us with the theological argument that the values of the reign of God transcend those, for example, of the family. Indeed, there are indications that such conflicts occurred even in Jesus' own family (Luke 8:19-21, Mark 3:21, John 7:5). Some have suggested that verse 53 may reflect prominent roles played by women in the mission of the early church.

Preparation: This strong reading may suggest things you may not want to hear. Be open to new ideas.

Read 12:49-53: Read these verses carefully. You may want to go back to look again at the introduction before your second reading.

Reflection: Atlanta's Cyclorama offers a three-dimensional view of one of the great battles of the Civil War. Included is a poignant scene where a dying soldier is ministered to by his blood brother on the battlefield. One is a Union soldier, the other a Confederate. There are similar stories of families divided over religious issues. Perhaps you know of such stories from your own experience. How do *you* understand the statement that Jesus came not to bring peace, but division? Do you have faith convictions that are strong enough to cause such fractures in your relationships?

Prayer: Ask God to help you with the feelings you have after praying these verses.

Why can't you read the signs of the times?

Commentary: Luke continues his urgent appeal to his readers in verses 54-56. Those addressed here are the multitudes in Jesus' time or, from Luke's perspective, members of the early church whose enthusiasm for discipleship has declined since their initial experience. In the twentieth century we might call them "backsliders" or "lukewarm Christians." The point is that we are all accustomed to predicting tomorrow's weather by looking at today's sky. But we overlook or ignore the "signs of the times" that God shows us in the life and teaching of Jesus.

Preparation: Before you center yourself to pray this reading, pause a moment to reflect on what you think Jesus might say or do if he were to be interviewed on your favorite evening news program.

Read: 12:54-56: Read these three verses; pause to recall the way you look at the sky and interpret what it means for the next few hours or the next day; then read it a second time.

Reflection: At one time or another most of us find ourselves sufficiently attracted to a cause, organization, or movement that we decide to become a part of it. It may be an environmental concern, a women's organization, a parent-teacher association, or neighborhood improvement group. We sense the urgency or importance of the need and offer our enthusiastic support. But over a period of time our enthusiasm wanes, and we find ourselves less and less involved, perhaps giving only lip service when we formerly gave our time and money. Is it any different in the church? What has happened to your sense of urgency about being a follower of Jesus Christ? What are the "signs of the times" as you read and pray the gospel . . . and as you read and pray the daily news headlines?

Prayer: Be honest about your own reading of the signs of the times. Ask God to stir up in you a new enthusiasm for who Jesus is in your life and in the life of the world.

[147]

LUKE 12:57-59 (TEV)

Settle the dispute . . . before you get to court

Commentary: Having warned his readers about the divisions that come as a result of Christian discipleship and of the importance of not misreading the signs of the times, Luke continues with a plea to settle one's disputes before it is too late and one is dragged into court. Once a case comes to court, the parable says, all that remains is the sentencing. The meaning is clear. Christians are urged to pay attention to their relationship with God before it is too late. When Matthew uses this parable to illustrate Jesus' teaching about anger, the emphasis is on settling disputes and bringing about reconciliation with neighbors (Matthew 5:25-26). Jesus has already connected the love of God and neighbor in relationship to salvation. Thus there would seem to be little difference between the application of the parable in the two Gospels. What is important is the urgency of reconciliation.

Preparation: Let your preparation for prayer involve awareness of any unfinished business you may have in your relationship with God, a friend, neighbor, co-worker, or family member.

Read 12:57-59: Read this brief passage in Luke. After a moment or two turn to Matthew 5:21-26, and read it also.

Reflection: Here is another example of gospel values turning the values of the world upside down. You may have heard the advice repeated at the end of the popular TV court program which says, "if you have a dispute with someone, take 'em to court." Jesus says, if you have a dispute with someone (or with God), settle it out of court. The author of Ephesians agrees, saying in effect, "it's normal to be angry, but settle your problem before the day is out so that it doesn't lead you into sin" (Ephesians 4:26). How do you usually deal with such things? What would you need to do to heed the urgent advice offered in this reading?

Prayer: Confess to God any problems you feel you have in handling your relationships with God or others. Ask for guidance to help you "settle out of court."

Do you think it proves that they were worse sinners?

Commentary: The theme of judgment has been a part of the past several sections. We now hear the call to repentance. Jesus is asked about a recent event in which some people from Galilee were killed in what may have been some kind of civil disturbance near the Temple treasury. The implication is that they died because they were sinful people. Jesus' answer recalls another recent incident in which eighteen people from Jerusalem were killed in the collapse of a tower near the pool of Siloam. Again we are given no details but it may have been a construction accident. Jesus' point is that those who died in these incidents were no different, from the standpoint of sin, than those who remained alive. They just happened to have been in the wrong place at the wrong time. Those who raised the question have no grounds for assuming their own righteousness. All people must repent of sin.

Preparation: Pause a moment to take inventory of your body. Are there still places where you feel tension? Can you let go of it before continuing your prayer?

Read 13:1-5: As you read these verses, try to imagine the scene. Ask yourself why people came to Jesus with the question.

Reflection: Joseph Donders tells the story of an eleven-year-old boy told by an eye doctor that he needed glasses. The boy was very upset but wouldn't talk about it. Finally, the story came out. Two days before the exam he had found some men's magazines on top of an overloaded trash can and had looked at the nude pictures, even though he felt it was wrong. Thus, when told that he needed glasses, he thought, "God is punishing me. God is going to make me blind because of what I did."[48] How easily we jump to the wrong conclusions when something bad happens to us! We make the same mistake when we assume that God is rewarding us when something good happens.

Prayer: Enter into a dialogue with God about any assumptions you might make when good and bad things happen.

LUKE 13:6-9 (TEV)

Leave it alone . . . just one more year

Commentary: Since the beginning of chapter 12, Luke has woven together a series of teachings and parables with the effect of a powerful sermon on the theme of repentance and judgment. That sermon now concludes with the parable of the unfruitful fig tree, which has great appeal because it points both to God's judgment and God's mercy. It seems likely that this parable originally came from the same source as the fig tree parable told by Mark in 11:12-14, 20-25, and followed by Matthew in 21:18-19. Each uses it for a different purpose. While we cannot be certain which version is closer to the original, it would be in keeping with Luke's prophetic spirit for him to have recast Mark's version in order to temper the theme of certain judgment with the possibility of repentance and mercy. It was not unusual in the prophetic tradition for a prophet to intercede with God, asking for mercy on behalf of the people.

Preparation: Imagine yourself in church. A powerful sermon has just been concluded and the congregation is provided with a generous period of silence to absorb and reflect on it. Clear your mind of anything that distracts you.

Read 13:6-9: Try reading this parable three times. Read it first as if you were the fig tree; read it a second time as if you were the gardener; then read it a third time as the owner of the garden.

Reflection: What did you feel as the fig tree? What did you feel as the gardener who appealed for more time to give the tree special care and attention? What did you feel as the owner of the garden who expected his tree to produce fruit? In which role did you feel most/least comfortable? Why? Can you relate any of these feelings to experiences you have had in your life? What are the implications of this parable for those persons and programs over which you have some degree of power?

Prayer: Share with God the feelings you have about judgment and mercy as they relate to your own situation right now.

Any one of you would . . .

Commentary: This episode may be partly an example of the blindness and hypocrisy referred to in 12:54-56. But it may have another meaning. This is the last time in Luke that Jesus appears in a synagogue. Given the confrontational nature of the incident and its occurrence on the journey to Jerusalem, it may be Luke's way of signaling Jesus' break with the old order and the establishment of the church. The incident reminds us of the two stories in 6:1-11, both bearing on the question of the Sabbath laws. Note that the woman does not ask to be healed; the initiative comes from Jesus himself. The controversy provoked not only the question of healing on the Sabbath, but a power struggle between Jesus and the leader of the synagogue. Rather than confront Jesus with his anger, the official chastises the people present, who may also have come hoping to be healed. While this would be consistent with his role as synagogue leader, it may also indicate his reluctance to challenge Jesus' authority. The people clearly side with Jesus. Finally, note the imagery of the woman having been "kept in bonds" for eighteen years and now "released," as anyone would untie a donkey to give it water. Luke may be referring to those who have long been bound by the strictness of the Law and their need to be released without delay.

Preparation: Relax; be still; take time; release tension; breathe deeply; dismiss distracting thoughts; prepare for a good story.

Read 13:10-17: Take time to pause and imagine the scene: picture the synagogue, the woman bent over, the angry official, and the reaction of the people. Now read it again.

Reflection: What details did you notice when you pictured this incident in your mind? What is really going on here? Is there something in you that has been kept in bonds for eighteen years? Do you think God wants to release it, without your even asking?

Prayer: Ask God to help you become aware of something in your own life that needs to be released.

LUKE 13:18-21 (NRSV)

What is the Kingdom of God like?

Commentary: Both Matthew and Mark contain the parable of the mustard seed, and Matthew also has the parable of the yeast. But each places them in a collection of other parables. Luke, on the other hand, uses them in the midst of Jesus' journey to Jerusalem to help interpret other events. The message is that small beginnings can grow into great results. They serve to reinforce the previous story about the healing of the woman in the synagogue, a relatively minor event, yet one that symbolizes the end of the old order and the beginning of the reign of God. These parables also remind us not to be discouraged over what may seem to be failure, or at what may seem to be an immense task. Mustard seed and yeast, like the reign of God, have the power to grow into great things. Once more in adjoining parables Luke has offered us examples that come from the experience of a man and a woman.

Preparation: If you have a package of seeds available and/or a package of yeast, place them before you now to remind you as you pray of the power of small things to produce large results.

Read 13:18-21: Read these simple parables, remembering some of your own experiences with seeds and yeast.

Reflection: If you have a seed available, take time now to find a pot and some soil. Plant the seed(s) and place them in a place where you can watch them over the next few weeks and thus be reminded of the reign of God. How many growing things can you think of in your house or apartment? Think beyond your plants and even to the mold growing in the basement! Do you have potatoes or onions sprouting in the pantry or fresh garlic in the refrigerator? What is there inside you that continues to grow or ought to?

Prayer: Ask God to take the small things you are doing and let them become great in God's reign. Ask God to help you be aware of small things that grow to be great things.

Do your best to go in through the narrow door

Commentary: This unit opens with another reminder that Jesus is on his way to Jerusalem. What follows also reminds the reader that those who would enter the reign of God must be serious about their own journey. An anonymous question asking if only a few will enter the kingdom is answered indirectly with teachings drawn together from various sources. The answer might be summarized in the words of an old spiritual, "Ev'rybody talkin' 'bout heaven ain't goin' there." The door image in verse 24 means that one must be prepared to sacrifice to enter the kingdom. A second door image in the following verse means that the opportunity to enter will not last forever. Verse 26 is aimed at those we might call "namedroppers." Simply having shaken Jesus' hand, had lunch in his presence, or heard him teach in person doesn't constitute discipleship. Such persons will be surprised to find themselves rejected, while foreigners and even sinners are welcomed into God's reign!

Preparation: As you get ready to pray, be aware of the silence in and around you. Is it a friendly silence? Do you relax in it?

Read 13:22-30: After reading these verses, you might want to read the introduction again in order to be more comfortable with the somewhat disjointed flow of verses from several sources.

Reflection: If you have been praying Luke's Gospel in its natural order, perhaps you have a sense of being on the journey to Jerusalem. This reading is a challenge for us to take that journey very seriously. We are participants with Jesus and not merely those who go along out of curiosity. We are reminded that to be a part of the reign of God, we must be disciples. It is like a sign on a nursery in Ontario that says: "The best time to plant a tree was twenty-five years ago; the second best time is today." Today may be for us the second best time to go through the narrow door.

Prayer: Ask God to help you understand how you are called to take part in the journey to Jerusalem.

As a hen gathers her chicks under her wings

Commentary: "Some Pharisees" warn Jesus that he should get out of Galilee because Herod wants to kill him. Not always hostile, the Pharisees sometimes invited Jesus to dinner (7:36, 11:37, and 14:1). Some even acted as a moderating influence in the High Council, as in Acts 5:34. Even Paul, near the end of his ministry, continued to call himself a Pharisee (Acts 23:6). On the other hand the warning is not necessarily friendly. In 11:53-54 the Pharisees are said to be laying traps for Jesus. The warning could have been part of a conspiracy with Herod Antipas to "get the troublemaker out of Galilee."[49] If so, Jesus' response is Luke's way of saying that the journey to Jerusalem must be completed according to God's will. The double reference to "three days" suggests the resurrection. Jerusalem was often the site of confrontations between prophets and those who opposed them. Thus, Jesus' lament over the city, which might be more appropriately located in the passion narrative, as it is in Matthew. It reflects Jesus' love for Jerusalem and its people, as well as his desire to see Jerusalem repent and welcome the reign of God.

Preparation: Remember that in praying scripture you join in a tradition of Christian prayer that goes back at least 1500 years!

Read 13:31-35: First, try to get a sense of the various themes that are woven together. Then read it again to hear the message about the journey continuing to Jerusalem.

Reflection: Read verse 34 again. Have you noticed similar images in the Psalms that speak of protection under God's wings (Psalms 17, 36, 57, 61, 63, and 91)? Compare this passage with Luke 19:41-44. Have you ever had similar feelings about a city, a group, or a person? What do these readings say to you about God's desire for us to hear the Word and do it? Who would you like to "gather under your wings"?

Prayer: Can you allow yourself in your prayer to be tucked under the wings of God?

Does our Law allow healing on the Sabbath?

Commentary: These teachings occur while Jesus is a dinner guest in the home of a leading Pharisee. But this is much more than "table talk." Why does Luke include them? The issue of healing on the sabbath has already been dealt with in 6:6-11 and 13:10-17; and with respect to the next unit, Jesus had already made it clear that his ministry included poor people and outcasts. As Robert Karris says, "Luke explores Jesus' rich image of table fellowship to admonish the prosperous and smug of his [Luke's own] community."[50] In other words, the issues dealt with in these teachings were still being raised by the churches Luke was writing to. Verses 1-6 reflect either continuing tension between church and synagogue in Luke's time or similar tension between Jewish and Gentile Christians within the church over the issue of the sabbath tradition. The conclusion to be drawn is that caring for genuine human need transcends the law of sabbath rest.

Preparation: The sabbath day was to be a day unlike other days: a day for rest, refreshment, and fellowship with family and friends. Can you make your prayer such a time with God?

Read 14:1-6: Try to imagine the dinner in the home of the Pharisee with Jesus and other invited guests. Then remember the tension in the early church over similar issues.

Reflection: Can you think of modern social customs that have almost taken on the force of law in our lives? What things have become so rigid for us that we refuse to bend them for the good of someone in need? What about our taboo against picking up hitchhikers? What about our habit of not smiling or saying hello to a stranger we meet on the street? What about the competitiveness of our educational system that discourages children from helping each other to learn? What would Jesus have to say about such things?

Prayer: Ask God to help you see the rigid things in and around you that prevent you from caring for the needs of other people.

All who exalt themselves will be humbled, and those who humble themselves will be exalted

Commentary: To the healing story which takes place in "the home of one of the leading Pharisees," Luke now appends three teachings that seem to deal with table fellowship but are really meant to focus on the reign of God. Notice that the first is addressed generally to the guests present, the second to the host, and the third to an anonymous guest whose comment again calls attention to God's reign. The teaching in 7-11 is really an expansion of Proverbs 25:6-7. It closes with what some have called "the great reversal." By choosing the lowest place for ourselves, God will call us to a higher place. Once more, gospel values serve to turn the world's values upside down.

Preparation: Remember a time when you visited a particularly beautiful church or cathedral. Can you recall how you felt as you entered? Remember that time now as you get ready to pray.

Read 14:7-11: Be present at the scene of this teaching. Perhaps it will remind you of a seating problem you have experienced. Read it again, relating it to the entrance into God's reign.

Reflection: If you have ever been invited to a large banquet perhaps you will remember your feelings as you arrived and wondered where you would be most comfortable sitting. Have you observed people in such a situation who seemed to be "jockeying for position"? Have you listened as others engaged in name dropping to make themselves look important? What about those who dress to be noticed? What is your reaction to these kinds of social behavior? Many of us tend to see through such pretense and think less of those who engage in it. What kinds of things do *you* do or say to jockey for position? What might others think of you?

Prayer: Let God hear any feelings you may have experienced as you reflected on this teaching of Jesus. Ask for guidance concerning your own behavior.

When you give a dinner, invite the poor

Commentary: Having addressed the motivation of the guests, Jesus now turns to the motivation of the host. Being a host or hostess calls to mind graciousness, hospitality, and consideration. But one can also receive guests in order to gain power over them, especially if they are in no position to reciprocate. In the reign of God the host can never be repaid. The teaching thus calls us to extend our hospitality to everyone, especially to those who are poor, crippled, lame, and blind. We hear echoes of the social creed announced by Luke in Mary's Song and in Jesus' quoting of Isaiah 61 in Nazareth. Craddock reminds us that the New Testament word for *hospitality* means literally, "love of a stranger" and that hospitality is more than "having each other over on Friday evenings" or sending food to those who need it. In the reign of God, "the host and the guest sit at table together."[51]

Preparation: Take a moment to remember a time when you felt overwhelmed by the gracious hospitality of another person. Can you sense God's hospitality now as you get ready to pray?

Read 14:12-14: Before reading these verses, read Mary's Song in Luke 1:51-53 and Jesus' sermon in 4:16-21.

Reflection: The radical nature of this teaching cannot be overstated. Once more the values of the world are turned upside down by the values of the reign of God. In a time like our own it may be necessary to institutionalize our response to those who are poor and hungry, especially when we are called to act globally. But what about those who are our neighbors? Does the establishment of a neighborhood food pantry meet Jesus' standard for hospitality? What about our response to those who are homeless, jobless, or without adequate medical care? What else is necessary for our hospitality to truly be the "love of a stranger"? How many of us know the blessing of serving those who are not able to pay us back?

Prayer: Let your wrestling with these questions be your prayer.

They all began to excuse themselves

Commentary: This parable enlarges on the idea of hospitality in 12-14. It assumes the custom in which a person giving a banquet offered two invitations, one in advance, and another immediately before the banquet. Though difficult for us to understand, it was not unusual for guests to decline the second invitation due to a change in circumstances. The excuses given in verses 18-20 would have been honored at the time. For example, recent marriage was considered a legitimate exemption from military service. But in this parable the host is God, and no excuse, however valid by human customs, is good enough. Thus the host replaces the guests with the poor, crippled, blind, lame, and even passing strangers. The parable can be heard as the early church reaching out to Gentiles, the poor, and oppressed. On the other hand it can be a prophetic statement to a church (including many in our own time!) that has become so much a part of the establishment that it no longer seeks to include such persons in its fellowship.

Preparation: Some years ago a poster proclaimed, "If you're too busy to pray, you're too busy!" If you make excuses for not praying regularly, examine yourself in the light of this parable.

Read 14:15-24: Imagine the situation described. Then read it again, remembering that Jesus is describing God's banquet.

Reflection: This parable is difficult to appreciate apart from the social customs of Jesus' time. But we also need to acknowledge some of our own patterns about excuse making. How many of us are completely honest about declining invitations? How often do we tell socially acceptable lies to avoid doing something we simply don't want to do? "I have a previous commitment," "I don't feel well," "I'm expecting company," etc. What excuses do we make when offered opportunities to reach out to the poor and oppressed?

Prayer: Pray to the One who invites you to share in the heavenly banquet that you may be worthy to participate without excuse.

Whoever does not carry the cross

Commentary: The discussion about the reign of God continues, but now we are standing outdoors in a large crowd around Jesus. There is great enthusiasm but little understanding of what it means to follow him. Thus the theme is the cost of discipleship. Note the literary device repeated in verses 26, 27, and 33: "You cannot be my disciple unless. . . ." The NRSV accurately uses the word *hate* in verse 26, but we need to understand it as Semitic hyperbole (exaggeration) having to do with the ability to detach one's self from family for a more important cause. As LaVerdiere says, "the followers must consequently share Jesus' attitude of total self-giving, placing the life of others ahead of their own from every point of view."[52] Two brief parables illustrate the question Jesus raises, "when faced with a major expenditure of time, property, and life itself: Does this cost more than I am able or willing to pay?"[53]

Preparation: Has your prayer become *too* routine? Perhaps you need to change something, try a new place, or a different time.

Read 14:25-33: Read the three "whoever . . . unless" statements in 26, 27, and 33. Then read the entire passage at least once.

Reflection: Have you ever been caught up in the enthusiasm of a crowd and later realized the degree of commitment or sacrifice needed to follow through? Have you ever launched into a project that seemed like a wonderful idea only to discover that you lacked the resources to complete it? Imagine the enthusiasm and the parade atmosphere of the crowds around Jesus. Perhaps they thought all they had to do was follow him to Jerusalem and reap the benefits after he "confronted the establishment." This passage reminds us that following Jesus is a way of life that demands the highest commitment. What are the implications for your life?

Prayer: Begin by confessing your part in the "crowd mentality" around Jesus. Ask God to help you understand the real meaning of discipleship and give you the courage to undertake it.

If salt has lost its taste . . . they throw it away

Commentary: At first glance, the saying about salt seems almost unrelated to the content of the previous verses. Matthew uses the image of salt, along with that of light, to represent the Christian's example to others (5:13-16). Mark uses the saying about salt to represent friendship and peace in the church (9:50). In Luke, however, salt becomes a sign of committed discipleship, including the renunciation of anything that holds one back from following Christ. Thus it reinforces the meaning of verses 25-33. Just as salt can lose its taste, so can the early enthusiasm of discipleship fade over the course of time. And when the going gets tough it can also fade quickly, as Peter discovered in the short time between his promise of faithfulness in the upper room and his denial in the courtyard of the High Priest!

Preparation: If you have access to salt as you begin your prayer, place a few grains on your tongue to remind you of its special qualities. Recall how bland certain foods are without it.

Read 14:34-35: Read these two brief verses in the light of the commentary above. After a few moments read them again, and then go back and read verses 25-33.

Reflection: Take a few minutes to recall some of the "strong" moments in your life as a follower of Christ. Under what circumstances has your own witness been "salty" as you stood up for what you believed? What was the cost? Have there been times when you felt deeply committed around some issue and then saw your commitment fade with time? How do you see the salt of faith in other persons? How do you see it in yourself right now? Leave some salt in the place where you usually work as a daily reminder of your commitment.

Prayer: Ask God to take away anything bland in your faith and make you a salty Christian.

This man welcomes sinners and even eats with them

Commentary: This brief narrative serves as an introduction to three parables about the joy of recovering something that was lost. The introduction calls attention to two groups. First are the tax collectors and other sinners. That they represent every kind of outcast is made clear by Luke's use of the word *all* in verse 1 (NRSV). The second group is made up of Pharisees and scribes, symbolic of all who are self-righteous. It is the reaction of the second group to the presence of the first that sets the stage for the three parables. But it is not just the *presence* of sinners that upsets the scribes and Pharisees; it is the fact that Jesus welcomes them. Luke's purpose, of course, is not merely to report on such conflicts in Jesus' time, but to address the question of who should be welcomed at the table of the Lord in the early church. As LaVerdiere says, "as in Jesus' day, the openness and universality of that fellowship was being challenged by the self-righteous who protested the presence of sinners."[54]

Preparation: Remind yourself that God welcomes you when you pray, no matter what your condition.

Read 15:1-2: Imagine the people crowding around Jesus. Read these two verses from the point of view of the "sinners"; then read them again as if you were one of the Pharisees; then read them a third time, trying to hear what Jesus might have heard.

Reflection: With whom did you most identify in this scene? Are there "outcasts" in your church whose presence makes you uncomfortable? If so, why? What do you do to make them feel welcome . . . or unwelcome? What should you be doing with regard to them? Can you remember a time when you felt uneasy about going to church because of something you did? What happened? What could you and your church do to reach out to people who for various reasons may not feel welcome?

Prayer: Address your prayer to the God who welcomes you and all sinners unconditionally.

I am so happy . . . . Let us celebrate

Commentary: Luke makes it clear in verses 1-2 that the grumbling of the scribes and Pharisees is due, not just to the fact that outcasts came to Jesus, but that he received and even welcomed them. Jesus' response comes, not in confrontation or debate, but in parables that offer the self-righteous grumblers a non-threatening way to view the matter in another light. All three parables call for rejoicing when the lost has been found. The parables of the lost sheep (found also in Matthew) and the lost coin are almost identical in structure. One wonders if perhaps Luke added the latter because of its appeal to the experience of women. The sheep and the coin are both sought until they are found, at which time the rejoicing is so great that it must be shared with others. The stage is set for the third parable in which the rejoicing is not over an animal or an object but a person!

Preparation: Does your experience of prayer usually lead to rejoicing because you have found something?

Read 15:3-10: Read these two parables first to become familiar with their details and similarity. Then read them again to hear and feel the response of those who have found what was lost.

Reflection: Who among us has not had the experience of losing something? Perhaps in our time we ought to tell a parable about the lost keys, the lost comb, or the lost cash register receipt! How quickly the frustration of fruitless searching turns to joy when we finally find what we are looking for. How incomparable must be the joy of God when one of us who was lost is found! Should we not cultivate this kind of joy in our daily lives? Wouldn't it be wonderful if we celebrated the victory of a child who has learned from a mistake, rather than saying, "I hope you have learned your lesson"? Should we not rejoice every time a "sinner" asks for help?

Prayer: Share with God a time when you were "lost" and the response of others and yourself when you were "found."

Let us celebrate with a feast

Commentary: "The Prodigal Son" may be the best known and loved of all Jesus' parables. Repeated readings continue to surprise us with new insights. It is so well crafted that we need little help understanding it. By law the younger son (assuming the father had but two sons) would have been entitled to one-third of his father's estate.[55] (See also Deut. 21:15-17.) Verse 15 illustrates the extent of the younger son's degradation, because pigs were considered unclean. The "bean pods" (fruit of the carob tree) were used to feed animals and were only eaten by people in dire poverty.[56] Part of the parable's genius is the fact that both the "sinners" and the "self-righteous" could recognize themselves in it without feeling personally attacked.

Preparation: Silence can be either a hindrance or a gift to prayer. Take time to convert your *empty* silence into a *full* silence; your *anxious* silence into a *peaceful* silence; your *restless* silence into a *restful* silence.

Read 15:11-32: Read the parable, entering into it, as if you were reading it for the first time.

Reflection: Wouldn't it be more in keeping with the meaning of these parables to call them "the *found* sheep," "the *found* coin," and "the *found* son"? It is a comment on our human nature that we react to the latter by thinking, "Let the foolish young man return, but on his knees and with no reward." Perhaps this attitude comes from the grudging elder brother or sister in us. We forget that the father treated *both* sons with love and generosity. As Craddock says so well, "The embrace of the younger son did not mean the rejection of the older; the love of tax collectors and sinners does not at all negate love of Pharisees and scribes."[57] Why are we so offended by God's grace toward those whose conduct we consider questionable?

Prayer: Pray for greater ability to understand and offer to others the unconditional love that abounds in this parable.

Use money, tainted as it is, to win you friends

Commentary: Luke now offers us a parable about the proper use of money by Jesus' disciples—and Luke's readers. The parable of the shrewd manager, addressed to the disciples, properly ends at 8*a*. Verses 8*b*-13 are interpretive comments by Jesus and Luke. The parable is troublesome for those who hear the manager being praised for his dishonesty rather than his shrewdness. At least two interpretations are possible. Did he arrive at the smaller figures by dishonestly reducing the amount borrowed . . . or did he do it by subtracting the amount of his own commission?[58] In either case he created friends who might be able to do him favors after he lost his job. But looking only at the question of honesty is to miss the point of the parable, namely that the disciples, including Luke's intended readers, should use their wealth in ways consistent with life in the reign of God (verse 9). The sayings in 10-12, while relevant, are not dependent on the parable and seem to be drawn by Luke from various sources.

Preparation: Give yourself permission to simply enjoy the silence for a few minutes before going ahead with the scripture.

Read 16:1-13: Read the parable itself (16:1-8) twice and then read the interpretive sayings in 9-13.

Reflection: In the previous parable we were invited to forgive both the grudging older brother and the foolish younger brother in order to celebrate the latter's return. In this parable, dwelling on the manager's dishonesty may cause us to overlook the opening verse that describes him as wasteful (TEV) or squandering (NRSV). Are we not called to forgive him in either case and to celebrate the possibility of new life which resulted from his shrewd action? Which of us at one time or another has not been grudging, foolish, or perhaps even dishonest, when it comes to the stewardship of money . . . tainted as it is?

Prayer: Pray for the ability to manage the money you have in ways consistent with the values of God's reign.

You make yourselves look good, but God knows what is in your heart

Commentary: Our attention is now turned to the critical response to the parable by some Pharisees, who, feeling no conflict between their worship of God and their pursuit of riches, ridiculed Jesus' teaching as too unrealistic. Jesus answers by accusing them of being contemptible to God (verse 15). The next three verses have posed a problem for scholars because they *seem* to be out of context. It may be that they are Jesus' response to an assumed criticism from the Pharisees that his teaching waters down the Law of Moses. If so, the point is that the preaching of the good news about God's reign beginning with John the Baptist does not do away with the Law of Moses. If anything, Jesus says, his teaching is even more strict than that of the rabbis. This is illustrated by his teaching about divorce, which is far more strict than the traditional understanding based on Deuteronomy 24:1-4.

Preparation: Everything you do is part of your prayer, from choosing a text, to reading the commentary, to reading and reflection, and finally to conversation with God.

Read 16:14-18: You may wish to review the parable and comment in 16:1-9 before reading verses 14-18.

Reflection: The parables in 16:1-9 and 16:19-31 both have to do with the proper use of money by Jesus' followers. The Pharisees' difficulty seems to have been their *love* of money, the classic conflict experienced by the rich young man in 18:18-23. How much do *you* love money? Most of us don't consider ourselves rich, but wealth is a relative matter. If you have visited a third world country, you may have suddenly felt *very* rich. What then does it mean for you to manage your wealth with an eye to the values of the reign of God? These verses serve as an introduction to the parable of the rich man and Lazarus which follows.

Prayer: Pray for the ability to be honest with yourself as you evaluate your feelings about money and the way you use it.

If they do not listen to Moses and the prophets . . .

Commentary: The next parable about the proper use of wealth is a dramatic illustration of the reversal of fortunes in the Magnificat (1:53). The parable addresses the Pharisees' theology that their own good fortune was the result of divine blessing, a reward for their keeping the Law. In 19-26 the rich man, tormented by the fire of Hades, calls to Abraham to send Lazarus to comfort him. Later, the rich man asks that Lazarus, still thought of as an errand boy, be sent to warn his five brothers so they might be spared a similar fate. Abraham responds that the rich man's brothers have already been warned by Moses (the Law) and the Prophets. In a likely addition by the early church, the rich man continues to press for help, arguing that his brothers might pay attention if someone (Lazarus) were to rise from the dead. The parable thus speaks, not only to the Pharisees' misunderstanding of the Law and the Prophets, but also to the rejection of the risen Christ by those in the early church.

Preparation: As you breathe deeply as part of your centering, remember that the breath in you is, according to the creation story, the wind or spirit (*ruach*) of God breathed into you.

Read 16:19-31: In your second reading, note especially the two different requests of the rich man in 19-26 and 27-31.

Reflection: What prevented the rich man from going with Lazarus to Abraham? Was it his wealth or his assumption that his wealth was a sign of God's blessing and that the condition of the poor reflected their punishment by God? How many in our time take wealth for granted, yet blame the poor for being poor? It may be possible to justify the Pharisees' attitude on the basis of scripture, but only if we ignore the larger biblical tradition that calls us to share what we have with those who are less fortunate.

Prayer: Pray that who you are and what you have will not result in your being insensitive to either the values of your faith tradition or the needs of those around you.

If there is repentance, you must forgive

Commentary: Here Luke has skillfully woven together four otherwise unrelated teachings about life in the community. The first two (1-3*a* and 3*b*-4) address responsibility toward less mature members of the community and the need to forgive those who are repentant. Because members of the community possess differing levels of maturity, it is inevitable that some will stumble in their discipleship. But woe to those who *cause* others to stumble! Their deserved fate, as Jesus describes it, is sufficiently graphic as to need no explanation. Yet the second teaching suggests a balance, counseling that those whose sin gives offense to the community are to be "rebuked" (corrected) and offered *repeated* forgiveness.

Preparation: Pause to remember how your own sins have been repeatedly forgiven by God and by your family and friends.

Read 17:1-4: Even a brief teaching like this deserves special attention and repeated readings.

Reflection: Fred Craddock has written of these four verses:

> . . . the instruction proceeds on assumptions, some of which need to be discussed openly to determine whether they any longer prevail. For example, verses 3-4 assume the following: the relationships among disciples of Jesus are based on ethical standards, the violation of which is sin; what brothers and sisters do is not their business alone but affects the community; responsible love can both give and receive a rebuke; relationships in the Christian community can, with pain to be sure, generate and deal with repentance; words of forgiveness can be spoken and heard with no one seeming superior or trying to play God. These assumptions need to be discussed, claimed, modified, or replaced; it is difficult to imagine a faith community being formed and sustained in silence on these matters.[59]

Prayer: Let your prayer begin with your feelings about causing others to stumble and the repeated need for forgiveness.

[167]

Make our faith greater

Commentary: The teaching about forgiveness in 3*b*-4 had the same effect on the disciples (here called aspostles by Luke) that it does on many of us. How can we possibly forgive a person over and over again simply because he or she claims to be repentant? If that is what is expected, then we also need greater faith! The scholars are divided about the meaning of Jesus' response. Some interpret his, "If you had faith as big as a mustard seed . . ." as a condemnation of their lack of faith. But others, like Craddock, see it differently, pointing to two·different types of "if" clauses in the Greek language. The first expresses a contrary condition (if black were white) while the other expresses a condition according to fact (if water is wet). The "if" in verse 6 is of the second kind, meaning that the phrase could be translated, "if you had faith as big as a mustard seed [and you do], you could say . . . ." Jesus is thus affirming the faith the disciples do have and urging them to live by it.[60]

Preparation: Ask God to be part of your centering and prayer and to help you to live according to the faith you already have.

Read 17:3b-6: Include 3*b*-4 in your reading. Read the whole passage again.

Reflection: How does one measure faith? How much faith do you have? Have you ever discovered that in the midst of a crisis, you had more faith than you thought previously? Does that mean that our faith lies dormant much of the time waiting for a crisis? Or does it mean that we choose not to call on our faith except in emergency? What do we call on instead: our own resourcefulness? reason? luck? How might you increase your ability to exercise the faith you already have? What might you do to increase your faith?

Prayer: Let your reflection on these questions be the beginning of your prayer.

We have only done our duty

Commentary: While it is difficult to find a sense of continuity between verses 5-6 and 7-10, both come from a source unique to Luke and were undoubtedly placed together intentionally. It is also difficult for us to grasp the meaning of the teaching about a servant's duty because of the obvious cultural differences between our own time and Jesus' time, when the idea of servanthood was not only acceptable, but common. Verses 8-9 seem particularly cruel and unfeeling to us. The meaning, coming after the teaching about minimal faith, would seem to be that what Jesus has asked of his disciples is no more than one should expect of those who have chosen to serve him. They should expect no special gratitude for doing what is expected of them. Luke's message is that leaders in the church should likewise expect to serve without special attention.

Preparation: Do you see your prayer as a part of your "duty" as a servant of Christ, or do you expect God to be grateful to you for doing it?

Read 17:7-10: You will have to approach this teaching apart from our modern attitudes about slavery!

Reflection: Clearly we are called to be servants of Christ and servants of others. But have we fully understood what that means, or do we see it as an admonition to adopt a humble attitude? What does it mean except to find our lives by losing them? How are we to live without expectation of reward or gratitude for our work as servants? Can you think of yourself as undeserving of special attention after giving hours of your time for some worthy cause?

Prayer: Pray for greater insight into the role of servant to which you have been called.

Where are the other nine?

Commentary: This story begins with yet another reminder of the journey toward Jerusalem (see also 9:51-56; 10:38, and 13:22). The ten men suffering from a skin disease congregated outside the city gate where ritually unclean persons were allowed to beg for charity. By inference the group is composed of both Jews and Samaritans, who would not normally have associated with one another, but are here drawn together because of their common condition. Samaritans, like Jews, were obligated to follow the laws with regard to ritual purity though they went to an examining priest at their own temple on Mount Gerizim. The Samaritan's good example here may be Luke's way of anticipating what he reports in Acts, namely that while many in Israel were blind to who Jesus was, he was received by many others who were Gentiles.

Preparation: Begin by giving thanks to God for all that comes to you through prayer and for your many other blessings.

Read 17:11-19: As you read this story, let your mind imagine the setting described by Luke as well as the people involved.

Reflection: How easy it is to criticize the nine who were healed, but didn't return to say thank you. Perhaps we need to be reminded of the difference between gratefulness and thankfulness. Gratefulness is an inner attitude that exists prior to thanksgiving. It is possible that all ten were grateful for having been healed by Jesus. But being thankful is to move a step beyond gratefulness, as the author of Psalm 50 knew so well:

> *I do not need bulls from your farms*
> * or goats from your flocks. . . .*
> *If I were hungry, I would not ask you for food,*
> * for the world and everything in it is mine. . . .*
> *Let the giving of thanks be your sacrifice to God,*
> * and give the Almighty all that you promised."*(50:9-14, TEV)

Prayer: Let the giving of thanks be your sacrifice to God.

The reign of God is already in your midst

Commentary: When the Pharisees ask Jesus when the reign of God will come, his response is often translated, "the kingdom of God is within you." However, some have suggested that because the *you* is plural and because Jesus is speaking to the Pharisees who didn't accept his message, a more accurate translation is that "the Kingdom of God is already in your midst." Even so, he addresses the disciples in the following verse, warning about the suffering he and they will have to endure before the Son of Man returns. There will be nothing subtle about that time. It will be as plain as lightning that lights up the sky. It will come suddenly, and many will be unprepared. The way to be ready is not by trying to predict the time, a perversion of scripture that still continues in our own day, but by living in the knowledge that "the reign of God is already in your midst." When the disciples ask where this will happen, Jesus answers with the proverb about vultures gathering over a dead body. In other words the "where," like the "when," will be known only after it happens.

Preparation: Remember as you pray that the reign of God is all around you right now.

Read 17:20-37: This is not an easy passage to read or understand. Take plenty of time to read it slowly and carefully.

Reflection: This reading reminds us that the reign of God is both present and yet to come. Those who think only in terms of its future fulfillment are like teenagers who ask, "how will I know when I'm in love"? To think of it only as an event that will happen in the future is to miss the point entirely. Jesus is saying that those who live in the present according to the values of God's reign are those who will participate in its future fulfillment. Even in a world of conflict, violence, and racism, we are called to understand that the reign of God is already in our midst.

Prayer: Let us pray for ever-increasing ability to see the reign of God happening all around us.

Always pray and never become discouraged

Commentary: The teaching in 17:20-37 warns the disciples of Jesus (and Luke's readers) that they will have to endure suffering and oppression before the reign of God is fulfilled. Obviously such a message could lead to discouragement and to questions about when and how the "day of the Lord" will come. Thus Luke follows the teaching with two parables about prayer, the first advocating patience and persistence, and the second as a warning against self-righteousness among those who wait. The widow in the first parable is only asking for her rights as one of those offered special protection by Jewish law (see Deut. 24:17-22). The judge may have been corrupt, prejudiced, afraid of the widow's adversary, or simply lazy. In any case he finally grants her justice, fearing that she "will keep on coming and finally wear me out" (clearly she has already done so!). The point of the parable, and its parallel in 11:5-13, is that if such persistence can motivate the judge to act we should have no doubt about God's response to our persistence in prayer, even though it may seem like forever from our human perspective.

Preparation: Have you discovered that the quality of your experience in prayer is often related to the time and patience you give to it?

Read 18:1-8: Before reading this parable, go back and read its parallel in 11:5-13.

Reflection: Someone has observed that "time is nature's way of insuring that everything doesn't happen at once." Time offers us the opportunity to remember and reflect on the past as well as to look forward to the future. How strange that we often feel so uncomfortable with such a gift. One day we complain that "time flies" and the next we complain that "time drags on." Thus the need for persistence in prayer and for faith that we are not simply "hurling [our] petitions against long periods of silence."[61]

Prayer: Pray for greater patience and persistence in your prayer.

[172]

God, be merciful to me, a sinner

Commentary: The second parable on prayer could hardly be more direct in its confrontation of self-righteousness as an obstacle to spiritual growth. Luke's introduction leaves nothing to the imagination: Jesus "told this parable to some who trusted in themselves that they were righteous and regarded others with contempt." The Pharisee was the stereotypical example of righteousness carried to extremes. He thought of himself as deserving of God's special blessing. There was no reason not to believe his claims about fasting and tithing. The problem was that he was totally unaware of his own spiritual bankruptcy, his contempt for others notwithstanding. By contrast, the tax collector was deeply conscious of his own sin. It was such humility that made him and those like him open to God's forgiveness. Lest there be any doubt about the message of this parable (and how could there be!), Jesus interprets it himself, saying that it was the tax collector and not the Pharisee who went home justified in the sight of God. We can only imagine the reaction of the Pharisees who were present to hear this parable!

Preparation: Read this parable the first time before you center yourself to pray it, imagining the scene in the Temple.

Read 18:9-14: On your second reading, give special attention to your own feelings as you hear the prayers of the two men.

Reflection: The circumstances of our lives vary considerably over the span of many years. Who we are and what we bring to our praying may be very different now than it was at another point in our lives. At one time or another most of us have probably prayed like the Pharisee in this parable. Likewise most of us have prayed like the tax collector. As you look back over your own spiritual growth, what have you learned? What would you like to change about the way you pray?

Prayer: Allow God to help you take inventory of your own spiritual progress. Listen.

[173]

Whoever does not receive the Kingdom as a little child will never enter it

Commentary: As we have seen, Jesus concluded the parable of the Pharisee and the tax collector with a wisdom statement (found also in 14:11): "all who exalt themselves will be humbled, but all who humble themselves will be exalted." Luke now further illustrates the meaning of the parable by returning to the outline of Mark's Gospel from which he had departed with the beginning of the journey narrative at 9:51. The result is another example of Luke's skill in the ordering of his own Gospel. Jesus' blessing of the children and the story of the rich man who wanted to inherit eternal life serve to illustrate the spirituality of the tax collector and the Pharisee, respectively. It is the humble tax collector, not the proud Pharisee, who will be able to receive the reign of God like a little child. The attitude of the disciples toward those who bring their children to be blessed by Jesus makes it clear that they have not yet understood.

Preparation: Think about what it would mean for you to approach your praying "as a little child."

Read 18:15-17: As always, read the passage once, pause to continue in your centering, and then read it a second time.

Reflection: Some have rejected the conclusion that we are called to become childlike in our spirituality on the basis of the opening verse of this passage, which refers to those who were brought to Jesus for blessing as "infants" (NRSV) or "babies" (TEV, NEB, NAB). However, Jesus' use of the word *child* in the concluding verse would seem to include older children as well. What childlike qualities come to mind that might enhance the spirituality of adults? Trust; simplicity; directness; joy; wonder; lack of pretense; openness. How might such qualities enable your spiritual growth?

Prayer: Pray for a better understanding of this story and for the ability to "receive the reign of God as a little child."

Look, we have left our homes and followed you

Commentary: We call this story "the rich young ruler" because the synoptic gospels all call the man "rich." Matthew calls him "young," and Luke calls him "ruler." His motivation seems genuine enough, and there is no reason to doubt that he has kept the commandments. Or is there? Note that Jesus asks only about five commandments, all having to do with personal relationships. But what about the first and most important commandment, "You shall have no other gods before me"? That is "the one thing lacking" Jesus speaks about in verse 22. Here again the impediment is money, or more accurately, the idolatry of money. The saying about a camel going through the eye of a needle is hyperbole, an intentional exaggeration, to show that those who seek the reign of God must be prepared to sacrifice everything. Thus the response of Peter and the others who heard it! Jesus' statement that "what is impossible for mortals is possible for God" means that salvation comes from God and that God may find a way of breaking through one's idolatry.

Preparation: Insofar as regular prayer is participation in the reign of God, what are you willing (or unwilling) to sacrifice to make regular prayer possible?

Read 18:18-30: There is more to this story than meets the eye. You might want to consider praying it in two parts, 18-25 and 26-30.

Reflection: Imagine yourself in the crowd when the rich man expresses his desire to "inherit eternal life" (share in the reign of God). Can you feel his sadness as Jesus points out his addiction to wealth? When Jesus speaks about the camel going through the eye of a needle, are you one of those who responds, "Then who can be saved?" Can you hear Peter say, "Look, we have left our homes and followed you . . . what more do you want, teacher?" What is it in *your* life that keeps you from the reign of God?

Prayer: Ask God to help you discover what holds you back . . . and what you might do about it.

They did not grasp what was said

Commentary: We come now to the last of Jesus' three predictions about his death in Jerusalem (see also 9:22-27 and 9:43b-45). All three have parallels in Mark, where each is followed by a misunderstanding on the part of the disciples. Unlike Mark, Luke's second and third accounts are widely separated by the addition of the large body of independent material. While Mark's third account states that Jesus will be handed over to the chief priests and the scribes, Luke says he will be handed over to the Gentiles. There is another difference. The third prediction in Luke opens with the statement that the coming events in Jerusalem will happen to fulfill what the prophets have written. This is apparently the reason for Luke's addition of verse 34 in which the disciples' inability to understand is stated no less than three times! Fitzmyer sees this as preparation for the "opening" of the their minds by the risen Jesus in the Emmaus story (24:27ff) and in Jerusalem (24:44-45).[62]

Preparation: Pray for the opening of your mind to the scriptures as you prepare to read and pray these words.

Read 18:31-34: Read these verses slowly; pause; then read them a second time.

Reflection: Not only are the Gospels written from the point of view of the resurrection, but the reader is given clues and hints along the way. Thus we have an advantage over the disciples because we know the story. Even so, our eyes and ears continue to "be opened" each time we read and pray. How often have you read a portion of scripture and had the feeling that, "there is more to this than I am able to grasp"? And how often have you later come to understand it because of a new insight or clue you hadn't noticed before? There is much in scripture that is hidden from us until we are ready to understand.

Prayer: Give thanks to God that the scriptures are continually being opened to us.

What do you want me to do for you?

Commentary: In the verse preceding this story, the reader is told that the disciples "understood nothing" about the meaning of Jesus' prediction, that it was "hidden from them," and that "they did not grasp what was said." Now Luke follows with the story of a blind beggar who, because of his great faith, can "see" what others cannot see, namely that Jesus is the Son of David, the Messiah. It is another case of God's upside-down wisdom: the blind can see what those who have sight do not see! Coming near the end of Jesus' ministry, the story is a reminder that he indeed does have the power he claimed at the beginning of his ministry to bring about "recovery of sight to the blind" (4:18). Luke's telling of this story follows Mark's account with a few exceptions. One is his omission of the blind man's name, given by Mark as Bartimaeus. Another is Luke's statement that the encounter took place as Jesus *entered* Jericho rather than as he was *leaving,* as Mark says. The change was made necessary by the following story about Zacchaeus, which takes place *in* Jericho.

Preparation: We often do more than one thing at the same time—knitting while watching TV or drinking soda as we converse with a neighbor. But prayer calls for our undivided attention. Thus the need to put other things aside temporarily.

Read 18:35-43: Read this story first as if you were one of those in the crowd following Jesus. Then read it again, trying to hear it from the point of view of the blind man.

Reflection: Imagine yourself as the blind beggar. You hear the sudden commotion and ask, "What's going on?" They tell you it is Jesus of Nazareth. You have heard about him and want to get his attention. By what name or title do you address him? Those in the crowd tell you to be quiet, but you persist and he finally hears you and asks that you be brought to him. The crowd grows very quiet. Jesus says, "What do you want me to do for you?"

Prayer: Let your answer to the last question begin your prayer.

This man, also, is a descendant of Abraham

Commentary: In the last story a blind beggar found salvation in his encounter with Jesus. Now, from Luke's independent source comes the story of a *rich* man's salvation. Zacchaeus was not only rich, but, as a tax collector, an outcast! In fact he was the chief tax collector in Jericho, and thus responsible for the corruption of those he oversaw. But unlike the rich man in 18:18-30, whose love of wealth made his salvation impossible, everything about Zacchaeus speaks of his genuine sincerity: his desire to see Jesus (even to the point of climbing a tree); his hospitality; his repentance; and his willingness to go beyond what the Law required to repay those he may have cheated. Zacchaeus is Luke's way of illustrating the saying in 18:27 that, "What is impossible for mortals is possible for God." Salvation for Luke is more than conversion. It has personal, social, and economic consequences. Jesus' affirmation that, "this man, also, is a descendant of Abraham," could hardly have been lost on those in the "grumbling crowd." The final interpretation is Luke's own: "The Son of Man came to seek and to save the lost."

Preparation: Before you begin your centering, take time to imagine the setting of this story, including the crowd following Jesus through Jericho and Zacchaeus up in the tree.

Read 19:1-10: On your second reading, see if you can identify the feelings of Zacchaeus.

Reflection: Each of us has our own impediments that make it difficult for us to hear the gospel. But our attitude can make all the difference. Zacchaeus may have been the last person those in the crowd expected to find salvation. But he was eager to see Jesus, genuine in his spiritual search, and responded with "great joy" when Jesus called him. What attitudes do you bring that could determine your response to God's calling?

Prayer: Pray for understanding of the attitudes you bring to your quest for participation in the reign of God.

Invest this until I get back

Commentary: The final segment of the journey narrative has been variously called, "the parable of the gold coins," "the parable of the pounds," "the kingship parable," etc. It is related to the better known "parable of the talents" in Matthew 25:14-30. Luke's additions have the effect of making it into an allegory. Some scholars treat it as two interwoven parables, one about the stewardship of the ten servants, and the other (verses 12, 14, 15a, and 27) about a man who goes away to become king. Luke's overall purpose is to counter those who believed that the reign of God would begin almost immediately. The first parable encourages the church to remain faithful and continue Jesus' work during his absence. Verse 14 of the second parable reflects Archelaus' journey to Rome in 4 B.C.E. to receive the kingdom left by his father, Herod the Great. He was followed by a delegation of fifty Jews who went for the purpose of opposing him. Luke allegorizes this event to speak of the rejection of Jesus' kingship.[63]

Preparation: An important part of what we bring to the praying of the scriptures is faithfulness.

Read 19:11-27: This is a complicated parable/allegory. Begin by reading all the verses. Then go back and read verses 12, 14, 15a, and 27 to gain a sense of the second parable.

Reflection: Both parts of this parable/allegory address the question of Jesus "going away." The first is a reminder that it is not enough for those in the church to simply "hold the fort" until the reign of God is fulfilled with Jesus' return. Rather, we are to continue his ministry, witnessing to the world and bearing fruit. The second is a warning to those who may become discouraged or whose commitment to the gospel is halfhearted. The question of Jesus' absence and future return continues in our time. How do you feel about it? What are you doing while you wait?

Prayer: Pray for patience and faithfulness in your own discipleship.

Jesus' Ministry in Jerusalem
Luke 19:28–21:38

As he came near and saw the city, he wept over it, saying, "If you, even you, had only recognized on this day the things that make for peace! But now they are hidden from your eyes.
(Luke 19:41-42, NRSV)

THROUGHOUT THE TEN CHAPTERS OF THE JOURNEY NARRATIVE, Luke keeps Jerusalem before his readers as the final destination of Jesus' journey. At the beginning of the journey we are told that Jesus "set his face to go to Jerusalem." Scattered through the section are more reminders climaxing in 18:31 when Jesus says to the twelve, "Listen! We are going to Jerusalem where everything the prophets wrote about the Son of Man will come true."

Jerusalem and the Temple were vital to "Luke's understanding of the fulfillment of prophecy, the completion of Jesus' ministry, and the mission of the church."[64] In this Gospel, more than the others, most of Jesus' teaching activity in Jerusalem takes place in the Temple. The same is true of his confrontations with the religious establishment. This is intentional, as Luke himself notes in verbal brackets placed at 19:47 and 21:37. Based on the Gospel narratives, the church has traditionally assumed that the length of time between Jesus' triumphal entrance into the city and his resurrection was eight days. There are, however, various clues which lead some scholars to suggest a longer period of time, perhaps as much as several months.

If they keep quiet, even the stones would cry out

Commentary: Jesus' approach to Jerusalem was from the east through the town of Bethany. A short distance later the road bends around the southern brow of the Mount of Olives and then down the steep road, providing a magnificent view of the temple mount on the western side of the Kidron Valley. Luke follows Mark's account with some important differences. Verse 37 is added to describe the place where the loud praises began. The scene is more subdued with no crowd coming out to meet him as in John, and no laying of palm branches as in Matthew and John. Luke has the Pharisees ask Jesus to silence his noisy disciples, to which Jesus answers, "If they keep quiet, even the stones would cry out" (39-40). The meaning of Jesus' response is unclear. But, the road down the Mount of Olives was (and still is) lined with cemeteries. Could Jesus have meant that if his joyous disciples were silenced, even the dead would cry out?

Preparation: Let go of all other thoughts and concerns as you get ready to read to pray this powerful story.

Read 19:28-40: Use your imagination as you read these verses. Add your own details to the scene as Luke describes it.

Reflection: Take a few moments to remember all that has happened since Jesus was baptized and began his ministry in Galilee. Think about his preaching in Nazareth and his rejection by the hometown crowd. Remember his calling the disciples and his patience in training them. Remember his teaching over meals in the homes of Pharisees and his feeding of the five thousand. Remember the way he welcomed everyone who came to him. Remember his teaching about the reign of God and the cost of discipleship. Remember his "setting his face toward Jerusalem" and his predictions about what would happen there. Now the moment has come for him to enter the city. His disciples shout, "Blessed is the king who comes in the name of the Lord!"

Prayer: What do you feel? Can your feelings be your prayer?

If only you knew the things that make for peace

Commentary: Even as Jesus is hailed as king by his followers, we are reminded that he came also as a prophet. These verses, found only in Luke, provide a powerful dramatic contrast. While his disciples shout, Jesus weeps. While they sing, "Blessed is the king who comes in the name of the Lord," Jesus laments the city's blindness to its own fate. "If you only knew the things that make for peace" is both a commentary on the fate of the city about to reject him and a play on the name, *Jerusalem*, which means "vision of peace." Although the passage reflects Luke's knowledge of Jerusalem's destruction in 70 C.E., it may also reflect a tradition going back to Jesus himself.[65] It recalls Jesus' wanting to "put my arms around all your people, just as a hen gathers her chicks under her wings" (13:34-35). The lament will be reflected again in 23:26-32, as Jesus admonishes the women who weep as he goes to the cross, "do not weep for me, but . . . for yourselves and for your children." For Luke the destruction of Jerusalem was a result of its failure to accept the Messiah.

Preparation: Allow your mind to "descend into your heart" that you may pray these verses with your whole being.

Read 19:41-44: Listen first to the joyous shouts of the crowd; then on your second reading, try to understand what Jesus felt.

Reflection: Jerusalem's refusal to accept salvation when it was offered should not surprise us. When faced with a choice between change and inertia, most nations, like most individuals, are likely to opt for the latter, even if change holds the promise of a brighter future. And Luke has already warned us three times (6:26, 11:47, and 13:34) about the way Jerusalem treats God's prophets. Jesus' lament over Jerusalem has a timeless ring about it. How many prophets have lamented thus over modern cities . . . O Washington, "if you only knew the things that make for peace."

Prayer: Pray that you, your city, and your nation might yet hear and take seriously the words of the prophets.

My house shall be a house of prayer

Commentary: The cleansing of the Temple is reported in all four Gospels, although John, unlike the synoptics, places it near the beginning of Jesus' ministry. Luke has shortened the Marcan account to emphasize the importance of the Temple and make it the setting for Jesus' ministry in Jerusalem. There is no mention of his overturning the tables of the money changers as reported in the other Gospels, nor of Jesus driving the animals out of the Temple precincts as in John. The first part of the quotation in verse 46 is from Isaiah 56:7 and the second part from Jeremiah 7:11. Verses 47-48 not only emphasize Jesus' ministry of teaching and his popularity with the people, but also serve to foreshadow the passion. Thus begins the final confrontation with the religious authorities, who question and watch Jesus closely in the readings to come.

Preparation: How do you feel about the place where you pray? Does it feel like "a house of prayer"? If not, what might you do to make it so?

Read 19:45-48: Read this first to get a sense of all that Luke is telling us in the brief space of these four verses. Then read it again, trying to see in your mind the things he describes.

Reflection: Most churches are carefully designed and constructed to provide us with "sacred space" (sanctuary). Yet, with the passing of time and our increasingly casual attitudes about the difference between sacred and secular, a sanctuary can become an auditorium; prayer can become program; and worship can become entertainment. If Jesus were to visit your church today, what kind of space would he find? Would it be more like a house of prayer or "a den of robbers"? What about your personal prayer space?

Prayer: Ask God to increase your sense of sacred space, both spiritual and physical.

By what authority are you doing these things?

Commentary: By assuming his place as the authoritative teacher in the Temple, Jesus became an even greater threat to the Jewish leaders, especially to the scribes whose authority in matters of teaching was unquestioned. Thus Jesus was visited by a delegation from the high council (Sanhedrin), which was composed of the high priests, Pharisees, and elders representing major Jewish families. Given their position, the question they ask is understandable: "By what authority are you doing these things?" Their concern has to do with Jesus' cleansing of the Temple as well as his teaching there. Jesus, knowing that the motive behind the question was their seeking a way to destroy him, responds with a question of his own about the authority of John the Baptist. This becomes a dilemma for his questioners, as Luke clearly points out in verses 5-6. Their answer is not sincere, but merely a way of saving face in front of the people. The conflict between Jesus and the religious leaders will continue.

Preparation: As you prepare for this reading, pray that you will be open to recognize the proper authority of Jesus in your life.

Read 20:1-8: Read the passage slowly and carefully, imagining the scene as the people listen intently to Jesus' teaching. Feel the tension as the delegation from the high council arrives with its question.

Reflection: Have you ever asked yourself the question, "what authority does God have in my life?" How do you feel when you make decisions about your life and then sense something deep inside you questioning those decisions, calling you in another direction? What authority do you recognize in those situations?

Prayer: Pray for a better understanding of your personal freedom and for the grace to recognize the gentle, and sometimes not so gentle, nudging of the Spirit.

A man planted a vineyard, and leased it to tenants

Commentary: Having skillfully avoided a direct answer to the question posed by the religious leaders, Jesus continues with a parable addressed to the people, but clearly meant for the leaders who were still present. Luke has made the parable into an allegory, the meaning of which is not lost on its intended hearers (verse 19). The vineyard by tradition is Israel (Isaiah 5:1-7; Psalm 80:8-19), and God is its owner. The tenants in charge of it are the religious leaders; the servants sent to receive God's share of the harvest are the prophets; and the "beloved son" is Jesus. With the owner's response to the killing of his son, Jesus pronounces judgment upon the Jewish leaders and indicates that the vineyard will be turned over to new tenants, the Gentiles. Jesus is the rejected "stone" in the quotation from Psalm 118. As the story ends the leaders are furious but afraid to act because Jesus still enjoys the support of the people.

Preparation: As we go about our daily routines, we are seldom aware of the energy needed in order to function mentally and physically. Perhaps this is why we tend to neglect our spiritual needs. Centering offers us an opportunity to shift our energy from physical and mental activity to spiritual activity.

Read 20:9-19: You may want to go back and read verses 1-8 to remind yourself of the context of this reading.

Reflection: Think of yourself as one of the tenants in God's vineyard. What has God put you in charge of? What is expected of you? What fruit is produced in your part of the vineyard? What is God's share of the harvest? How do you treat those sent to collect what belongs to God?

Prayer: Pray for a better understanding of your role in the vineyard, and for clarity about any of the questions above.

Is it lawful for us to pay taxes . . . , or not?

Commentary: We can imagine the rage of the chief priests and scribes, outmaneuvered by Jesus' answer to their question and then humiliated by his parable. They wanted to arrest him immediately, but his continuing popularity with the people made that impossible. Unable to trap him on religious grounds, they looked for a way to trap him politically. To accomplish this they enlisted the help of spies whom they hoped Jesus would not recognize. After flattering Jesus with feigned compliments these persons went on to raise the question about paying taxes to Caesar. Recognizing the ploy, Jesus asked them to show him a denarius. Then, asking them to identify the coin (a Roman coin used for paying taxes), he told them to give to the emperor what belongs to the emperor and to God what belongs to God. He thus avoided the political trap laid for him and established a standard the church still uses to evaluate questions of church and state.

Preparation: Take whatever time is necessary to distance yourself from the issues and feelings of your day.

Read 20:20-26: This is not an easy teaching to understand. You may want to review the two previous sections or the commentary above before your second reading.

Reflection: The question asked of Jesus is a question the church continues to struggle with. Is it right to pay taxes, some of which may be used to support programs and policies Christians may consider to be unjust or oppressive? The dilemma is symbolized by the presence of a national flag in the sanctuary of many churches. What do you think Jesus would say about the divided loyalty implied by the presence of a flag alongside the cross in such sacred space? Which represents the ultimate loyalty of the Christian?

Prayer: Ask God to help you understand your commitment as a disciple of Christ, and the relationship of that commitment to questions of church and state.

God is not God of the dead, but of the living

Commentary: Although the Sadducees appear several times in Acts this is the only time Luke mentions them in his Gospel. They were conservative, aristocratic members of the priestly class who looked down on the Pharisees, whom they considered to be too modern in interpreting the Law. Although the Sadducees did not believe in a physical resurrection, their question is purely hypothetical, perhaps intended only for the purpose of argument or to divide the crowd. The first part of Jesus' answer says, in effect, that the question is irrelevant because, in the life to come, marriage will be transcended by a new kind of relationship. Then, recognizing that the Pentateuch was the only part of the Bible accepted by the Sadducees, Jesus appealed to their logic with an argument based on Exodus 3:6. If God is the God of the living and also the God of Abraham, Isaac, and Jacob, then the latter are living and not dead. His answer brings a compliment from some teachers of the Law who were there. However, the compliment is really political in nature since, in this instance, Jesus had come down on the side of the Pharisees.

Preparation: The image of going down a gently descending spiral staircase may be a helpful way of centering for prayer. With each step downward, leave distracting cares behind.

Read 20:27-40: As you read, remember the scene near the Temple and those present who listen intently to Jesus' words.

Reflection: Because the Gospels often paint a picture of Jesus in situations of conflict with the Pharisees, this passage reminds us that he probably had more in common with the Pharisees than with any other party within Judaism. The Pharisees were the progressive thinkers of their time. How often do we allow fine points of theology, biblical interpretation, politics, etc., to cloud our ability to see what is really essential?

Prayer: Ask God for the grace to be able to let go of nonessentials in order to be open to real growth in the Spirit.

[187]

LUKE 20:41-44 (NRSV)

How can they say that the Messiah is David's son?

Commentary: The compliment by the teachers of the Law breaks the tension, providing an opportunity for Jesus to ask the final question. In order to understand his question we must understand the problem posed for him by those who used the messianic title, "Son of David." That term carried with it various military and political images associated with King David. Because these images ran counter to Jesus' own understanding of who he was, there were many who did not take him seriously. He didn't fit their preconceived image of what the Messiah would be like, so how could he be the Messiah? Jesus thus appeals to an interpretation of Psalm 110:1 to argue that the Messiah is David's Lord, not David's son. Luke is saying that Jesus is not the military or political leader many people in his time expected.

Preparation: There is a sense in which centering means to empty one's self. Open yourself and let the tensions, worries, and agendas drain out of you. You can come back to them later when you are refreshed and are better able to deal with them.

Read 20:41-44: This is a very difficult passage to read and understand. If you still have trouble with it, you may want to consult one of the commentaries suggested in the bibliography.

Reflection: This teaching is helpful in explaining some of the tension we have encountered between Jesus and others throughout the Gospel. It may also help to explain some of our own hesitation in understanding who Jesus is. If we come to him with our own preconceptions, then we will be less able to hear who he really is. The problem is further complicated by the fact that over the centuries many Christians have been encumbered by theological baggage that Jesus himself would reject. What is the relationship between your own idea of the Messiah and the image of the Messiah presented in Luke's Gospel?

Prayer: Ask God to open you to a deeper appreciation of who Jesus really is.

The rich offered their gifts from what they had to spare

Commentary: Now Jesus speaks to his own disciples about the quality of leadership he expects of them. It is important to note that this is not a private conversation but one that takes place, "in the hearing of all the people," presumably including the teachers of the Law who were present. What is expected of the disciples is thus a matter of public knowledge. The disciples are not to conduct themselves like the teachers of the Law, who make a public show of their justice and at the same time take advantage of widows who come to them for help. This leads Jesus to contrast giving to the Temple treasury on the part of the rich with that of a poor widow who gave two coins of the smallest denomination. The standard Jesus uses is not the amount of their respective gifts, but rather what they had left after making their offering. The rich gave out of "what they had to spare," while the poor widow's offering, small as it was, consisted of everything she had.

Preparation: Recall one of the most relaxing and peaceful times in your life, perhaps when you were on vacation. Remember what it felt like as you ready yourself to pray.

Read: 20:45–21:4: After reading these verses the first time, go back and read them again, imagining the scene as the rich men and the poor widow drop their respective offerings into the Temple treasury.

Reflection: Once more we are offered an insight into the upside-down values of the reign of God. In human terms we often measure generosity by the face value of the gift. But according to Jesus' standard, generosity is to be measured by how much one has left after the gift is given! How do you make decisions about your own benevolent giving? Does it come off the top or do you give out of what you have to spare?

Prayer: Ask God to give you the grace of understanding this new idea of what generosity means.

LUKE 21:5-19 (NRSV)

Beware that you are not led astray

Commentary: We come now to what is often called "the Little Apocalypse" because of its focus on the end of the world as we know it, and the beginning of a new world. It may be a collection of isolated sayings of Jesus edited first by Mark and then by Luke in light of their knowledge of Jerusalem's destruction. The "signs of the end" (8-11) include warnings about false messiahs and predictions. War, revolution, earthquake, and famine are common occurrences in any age and do not necessarily indicate that the end is near; nor does the destruction of the Temple. Nothing here supports the so-called "doctrine of the rapture" that some today still confuse with apocalyptic theology. Verses 12-19, probably influenced by later events, serve as a warning to the church that it will face hardship and persecution at the hands of various authorities. Some will be "handed over" by family or friends but need not worry about defending themselves. They will be shown what to say and do. "Luke's concern is thus to interpret the destruction of the temple in relation to the end as well as to help Christians to respond adequately to their present difficulties."[66]

Preparation: It is not necessary to ask for God's presence; simply put aside distractions so that you can be present to God.

Read 21:5-19: A second reading of the commentary may help to understand this passage and the two that follow.

Reflection: Luke, following Mark, crafted this passage to speak to the needs of those in his own community who struggled to understand the meaning of the destruction of the Temple and with it, the city of Jersusalem. In parts it reflects Jesus' warning to his followers not to be led astray by false predictions and messiahs. Rather, one should remain faithful, avoid predictions, and witness to one's faith. It is still an important message amid all the false prophets and predictions of our own time.

Prayer: Pray for the strength and courage to remain faithful in a world filled with fearful events and signs.

When these things begin to take place . . .

Commentary: In verses 5-19 Luke told his readers not to see the destruction of the Temple as a sign of the end time. Rather it was to be seen as a reason to remain faithful and guard against false predictions and false messiahs while waiting for the new age to begin. That section now has its parallel in verses 20-28, which speak of the destruction of Jerusalem, likewise not to be understood as the beginning of the end, but as the beginning of the "time of the Gentiles," separating the "age of the Jews" from the coming of the Son of Man. Because the destruction of Jerusalem had already taken place when Luke wrote, verses 20-24 probably reflect his knowledge of the historical event rather than a detailed prediction by Jesus prior to its happening. The coming of the Son of Man in 25-28 is described in terms typical of apocalyptic literature and should not to be confused with the signs related to the destruction of Jerusalem in 20-24.

Preparation: If you feel anxious about the time needed to pray scripture, you might want to ask yourself how important prayer is to you. If it is important, then it deserves not only *enough* time but enough *quality* time.

Read 21:20-28: Again, the Little Apocalypse is not easily understood. You may need to read the commentary a second time before you continue with your reading and praying.

Reflection: It is difficult for us twenty centuries later to imagine the impact that the destruction of the Temple and of Jerusalem had on Luke's readers . . . even though most of them were Gentile Christians. Such things happen, Luke is saying to them, and should not be taken as certain signs that the reign of God will be fulfilled immediately. And yet they should call us "to stand up and raise our heads" because our salvation is near.

Prayer: Let us pray for the patience to wait for the day of the Lord's coming without growing complacent.

Be on watch and pray always

Commentary: The Little Apocalypse and Jesus' teaching ministry in Jerusalem come to an end with a call for the church to respond appropriately as it waits for the fulfillment of the reign of God. Just as summer is near when leaves begin to appear on the fig tree, the appearance of the cosmic signs (25-26) will signal the fulfillment of God's reign. All these things will take place in "this generation" (NRSV) or "before the people now living have all died" (TEV). The meaning is the same as the saying ascribed to Jesus in 9:27. But the "end time" did not occur accordingly, and the church has responded by interpreting "this generation" to mean humankind, thereby extending the time frame indefinitely. Nevertheless, the time will come (33), and Christians should "be on watch and pray always" in order to be ready. The section closes with a brief summary (37-38) which, like the summary of the journey narrative (19:47-48), offers a hint about events to follow. By calling our attention to Jesus' pattern of teaching in the Temple during the day and going to the Mount of Olives at night, Luke explains how the authorities will be able to arrest him away from the crowds that surrounded him every day.

Preparation: Take a moment to reflect on the contrast between the way you feel when you are centered for prayer and the way you feel in the midst of a hectic daily schedule.

Read 21:29-38: In your first reading pause briefly after verses 31, 33, and 36 to be aware of the four sections of this reading.

Reflection: One of Luke's purposes in writing his "orderly account" was to explain why the reign of God had not been fulfilled during the first generation of Christians. His answer is that we now live in an in-between time, the length of which is beyond our knowing. Instead of making fruitless predictions about the end, we are to live faithfully, watching and praying always. How do you feel about Luke's answer?

Prayer: Ask God to help you to "be on watch and pray always."

THE PASSION NARRATIVE
Luke 22:1–23:56

Father, if you are willing, remove this cup from
me; yet, not my will but yours be done.
(Luke 22:42, NRSV)

WE COME NOW TO THE PASSION NARRATIVE, which together with
the resurrection account comprises a disproportionately large
amount of space, not only in Luke, but in the other Gospels as
well. This is not surprising in light of the content of the preaching
and teaching traditions of the early church, which centered on
Jesus' death and resurrection. The outline of that tradition may be
seen in Paul's summary of his own preaching found in 1
Corinthians 15:1-8.

There is general agreement among the scholars that the
original core of the gospel tradition centered around these well-
defined accounts of Jesus' passion, death, and Resurrection. The
opposite is true of the birth narratives found in Matthew and
Luke, which were probably the last parts of the gospel to be
placed in written form.

The outline of the passion narrative consists of an
introduction (22:1-6) followed by three major blocks: the Passover
meal (22:7-38); the arrest and trial (22:39–23:25); and the
crucifixion, death, and burial (23:26-56). With relatively minor
omissions and additions Luke follows the Marcan narrative.
Luke's most important additions are the disciples' argument
about greatness and Jesus' response to it during the supper
(22:24-30); Jesus' advice to the disciples to be prepared for the
events about to happen by having with them "a purse, bag, and
sword" (22:35-38); and the hearing before Herod Antipas (23:6-
12).

The chief priests and the scribes were looking for a way to put Jesus to death

Commentary: With these six verses Luke begins his passion narrative, announces the place and time, introduces those who "were looking for a way to put Jesus to death," and establishes their motives—money in the case of Judas and fear of the people on the part of the chief priests and scribes. As the text implies, Jesus' popularity with the people constituted a threat to the religious leaders and also provided him with a certain degree of protection against them. Thus their need for secrecy. Judas is cast in the role of the traitor, even though the Gospels give no prior reason for his actions or clue to his lack of character. While various theories have been put forth to explain his decision, none is adequate. Suffice it to say that he represents the "dark side" in all of us.

Preparation: How much time have you allowed for your praying today? What would your reaction be if it took an additional fifteen minutes to pray it well?

Read 22:1-6: Try reading these verses out loud as if you were the narrator. Then go back and read them slowly and quietly to yourself.

Reflection: There is a strong sense of evil in these verses, beginning with the announcement of the plot and continuing with the motive (fear) of the plotters. Satan enters the scene. We react also to our previous associations with the name *Judas*. Then there is the word *betray* and the offer of money. What do you feel? What personal experiences are you reminded of? Is there a bit of Judas in you?

Prayer: Let your prayer flow out of your feelings and associations with the words in this text.

Go and prepare the Passover meal for us

Commentary: The synoptic Gospels all present the Last Supper as a Passover meal, while in John it occurs on the evening before the Passover. Luke adds a few details to Mark's account of the preparation for the meal. Mark doesn't name those sent to make the arrangements, but in Luke the discussion is initiated by Jesus, and Peter and John are assigned to the task. The detail about their meeting a "man carrying a jar of water" (water jars were usually carried by women) may be a sign of pre-arranged secrecy necessitated by the danger of Jesus entering the city at night when the absence of crowds might make him vulnerable to arrest. If so, the secrecy may have extended even to other disciples, since Jesus appears to have had prior knowledge that Judas would be the one to betray him. In any case, the room having already been arranged for, the tasks of Peter and John would have included purchasing the lamb and having it roasted, and buying the necessary bread, wine, herbs, and other food.

Preparation: Peter and John must have had a list of things to do to prepare for the Passover meal. Check your list of things to do as you prepare to pray. Have you forgotten anything?

Read 22:7-13: Use your imagination as Peter and John check out the upper room and do their shopping for the Passover meal.

Reflection: On the surface the assignment Jesus gave to Peter and John may seem like running errands. They had to make sure the room was adequate, shop for all the food, arrange to have the lamb roasted, etc. Yet this was no ordinary meal they were getting ready for. Surely they must have known, even as they shopped, that it would be Jesus' farewell banquet. Are you sometimes called upon to help prepare for a church supper or some other festive meal? What do you bring to such a task to make it a special occasion? What does "hospitality" really mean?

Prayer: Pray for help on those occasions when you are called upon to prepare something special for others.

LUKE 22:14-20 (NRSV)

This cup that is poured out for you
is the new covenant in my blood

Commentary: Joseph Fitzmyer begins his commentary on this passage with an excellent summary and an appropriate caveat:

> . . . Jesus celebrates the Passover meal and reinterprets it, sharing bread and wine with his apostles, giving these elements a new meaning, and instructing them to repeat such a meal in memory of him in future times. Though it seems to be a straightforward account,[67] "the Lucan account of the Last Supper is a scholar's paradise and a beginner's nightmare."[68]

Luke has altered Mark's order by moving the reference to Judas from the beginning to the end of the meal, thereby adding dramatic effect and also making Judas a participant in the ritual of the new covenant. Verses 19-20 are remarkably similar to 1 Corinthians 11:23-25. Some scholars believe these words probably came from a common source, possibly a liturgical tradition that would have been familiar to the Lucan communities.

Preparation: "Deep within us all there is an amazing inner sanctuary of the soul, a holy place, a Divine Center, a speaking Voice, to which we may continuously return."[69]

Read 22:14-20: Try not to let the profound meaning of this story be obscured by the complex problems related to its structure.

Reflection: Among the details not included are the place where the meal took place, its owner(s), those who prepared and served the meal, and the possibility that others in addition to the apostles may have been present. Imagine yourself one of the other persons present at the table or perhaps watching from the kitchen. Let your imagination provide additional details and conversation related to this pivotal event in the history of the church.

Prayer: Now the meal is over, the dishes are done, and Jesus and his disciples have gone to the Mount of Olives. You are the last one left in the room. In the stillness of the night offer your prayer.

[196]

The one who betrays me is with me

Commentary: Luke places the announcement of the betrayal immediately after the institution of the "Lord's Supper" to catch our attention. And it does! The response of those at the table is natural, as if to say, "which one of us could possibly do such a thing?" The discussion immediately turns to the question that had plagued the disciples earlier, "which one of them should be thought of as the greatest." Does this not constitute a form of betrayal by *all* the disciples, who seem to have forgotten having had the same argument in Galilee (9:46-48)? And have they not learned anything from Jesus' teachings in 14:7-11, 18:9-17, and 20:45-47? But the disciples are not the only people who struggle with this question. Luke is also addressing the leaders of the early church who also struggled with greatness and humility. In verses 25-30 the disciples and the church are again reminded that in the reign of God human values are turned upside down.

Preparation: Sometimes we come to prayer with intense feelings of anger, anxiety, or fear. If you are unable to let go of such feelings, offer them to God and ask for help in dealing with them.

Read 22:21-30: Go back and begin your first reading with verse 14 to sense the full impact of the setting. Then, after a pause, read verses 21-30.

Reflection: Imagine all the emotions that were present in those who shared the meal in the "room upstairs." Think of the questions that must have been on their minds! Suddenly, all of that was interrupted by the question of betrayal! Then fear, anxiety, and defensiveness gave way to self-justification in the dispute about who was the greatest. Once more Jesus had to remind his impetuous disciples that he had called them to a better way of life. Recall a few times when you have "flown off the handle," "lost your cool," or "blown it." How did you feel? What did you learn from the experience?

Prayer: Pray for the grace to grow in the spirit of Christ.

LUKE 22:31-34 (JB)

Satan . . . has got his wish to sift you all like wheat

Commentary: As the farewell banquet continues, it becomes more and more clear that the disciples have failed to grasp all that is happening. Even though one of them will betray him, and all have fallen into an argument about their own importance, Jesus has made them the new rulers of the reign of God (29-30). The use of "Simon" in 31-32 and "Peter" in 33-34 is but one indication that this unit is a Lucan composite. Jesus' warning that the power of Satan, already acting in Judas, will "sift all of you like wheat" (an allusion to Amos 9:9) means that the disciples will continue to be tested. Peter's lack of faith is singled out to impress on him the importance of his role as their leader. In spite of his affirmation of loyalty unto death, Jesus predicts his denial. Yet Peter will recover from it (32b) and must take seriously his responsibility to strengthen the others. All disciples, including those in the church, will have their loyalty and fidelity tested.

Preparation: As you prepare for this reading, ask God to open your heart to a greater appreciation of the faith struggles of your spiritual ancestors.

Read 22:31-34: During your first reading try to get a sense of what Peter was feeling; then read it again, concentrating on the perspective of Jesus.

Reflection: How easy it is to join some organization, movement, or cause and pledge our loyalty to it. But how quickly our enthusiasm diminishes when we are asked to do something. Every pastor knows how a new church member's excitement can diminish over the course of a few months or even weeks. But, unlike many pastors, Jesus refused to give up on Peter. The right kind of prayer and nurture can see a wavering disciple through the time of testing. Peter recovered, and so can we.

Prayer: Let your prayer be one of thanksgiving to the God who doesn't give up on you when you falter. Also ask for the faith that enables you to sustain others when they falter.

[198]

Enough of this!

Commentary: These verses, found only in Luke, bring the upper room conversation to a dramatic conclusion. Jesus makes one last attempt to impress on his disciples the importance of what is about to happen. He reminds them that when they went out on their own (9:3 and 10:4) they took nothing with them, depended entirely on the hospitality of others, yet they lacked nothing. But now they will have to rely completely on their own resources. Thus the symbolic remark about buying a sword. The disciples, however, fail to understand the symbolism and respond that they already have two swords! Jesus, by now impatient with their thick-headedness and ready to move on to the Mount of Olives, puts an end to the conversation with a terse, "Enough of this!" The quotation from Isaiah 53:12 in verse 37 is his way of saying that he will "share the fate of criminals" and, by implication, so will his disciples. That they did is reported by Luke in Acts 4:1-22.

Preparation: Many voices clamor for our attention. Tune them out, that you may be attentive to the One Voice that calls to you.

Read 22:35-38: After your first reading go back to read the commentary again. Then come back to this dramatic scene.

Reflection: The reference to "purse, bag, or shoes" recalls the sending of the seventy-two (10:1-12) rather than the sending of the twelve disciples (9:1-6). But the point is the same: the need to travel lightly, depending on others for hospitality. But now the situation is very different, and they will have to provide for themselves. The remark about buying a sword was symbolic, emphasizing his disciples' need to have their wits about them in the coming conflict. But the disciples, forgetting that the way of violence contradicts everything Jesus has taught, took it literally! How many in our own time make the same mistake, perhaps even using this reading to justify the sword?

Prayer: Pray for the spiritual maturity to meet the challenges that come in your life according to the ways taught by Jesus.

Why are you sleeping?

Commentary: Luke's account of Jesus' praying just before his arrest is brief compared to Mark's and contains several differences. The introduction serves to change the scene and establish the location which he calls the Mount of Olives, rather than Gethsemane. Jesus' words, "pray that you will not fall into temptation" (TEV), are repeated at the end of the passage to provide a literary frame. In Luke that instruction is addressed to *all* the disciples while in Mark, Jesus takes Peter, James, and John with him, telling the others to "Sit here while I pray." Matthew and Mark have Jesus returning three times to find the disciples asleep; in Luke it is only once. The disciples, however, will fall into several temptations, only one of which is the temptation to sleep. Verses 43-44 are not found in many of the earlier manuscripts and are probably a later addition to bring Luke's account closer to the description of Jesus' agony in Matthew (26:37*b*-38) and Mark (14:33*b*-34).

Preparation: If your pattern of prayer has become *too* routine, you may want to think about adding or changing something like the time, place, a candle, etc.

Read 22:39-46: Omit verses 43-44 in your first reading. Then include them in your second reading and note the difference.

Reflection: How often in the long journey with Jesus from Galilee to Gethsemane we have seen the disciples miss the point, misunderstand, or otherwise seem slow to learn! How hard Jesus tried in the dinner conversation in the upper room to get through to them! Now at the very hour of his passion and arrest, they can't even stay awake. Try to recall at least one time when you couldn't stay awake even though someone needed and depended on you.

Prayer: Pray that you may be alert when others need you and "that you will not fall into temptation."

The power of darkness

Commentary: "While he was still speaking," the chief priests and the elders, led by Judas, arrive with the Temple police to arrest Jesus. Luke's account is shorter than Mark's, omitting several details. Speaking first to Judas, Jesus recognizes both the act of betrayal and the fact that it is done with a kiss. The action then moves swiftly as the disciples, still not understanding Jesus' remark about swords, ask if they should strike. Then, not even waiting for an answer, one of them lashes out, cutting off the ear of the high priest's slave. (Only the fourth Gospel calls him Peter.) The sad irony of Jesus being betrayed with a sign of affection is now reversed as another disciple with genuine affection defends him with a sword! Jesus' immediate response, "No more of this!" echoes his rebuke of the disciples on the same topic as they left the upper room. After healing the slave's ear (a detail found only in Luke), Jesus turns to those who have come to arrest him. His reference to the "power of darkness" has a double meaning, referring not just to their evil conspiracy, but to the cowardliness of their acting at night when they don't have to answer to the people who surrounded Jesus in the Temple during the day.

Preparation: Ask yourself if you pray from a genuine desire to be in God's presence or out of a sense of duty or habit.

Read 22:47-53: Note that Jesus speaks three times, rebuking Judas, then the disciples, and finally the arresting party.

Reflection: The conspiracy against Jesus, conceived in "the power of darkness" and carried out under cover of darkness, has now infected even the disciples. Contrary to all they have learned from Jesus, they resort to violence in his defense. Thus surrounded by "the power of darkness," Jesus confronts Judas, the disciples, and those who have come to arrest him with the truth about themselves. Where is "the power of darkness" in you?

Prayer: Pray that the power of darkness in you might be brought to light in Christ.

I do not know him

Commentary: The prediction of Peter's denial only hours earlier is now fulfilled. If some of the details seem confusing it is because our minds form a composite picture based on all four Gospel accounts. In Matthew and Mark Jesus is taken inside the house of the high priest where a hearing is held before the council at night. Peter remains "below" (NRSV) in the courtyard. In John, Peter stands "outside at the gate" until arrangements are made for him to come into the courtyard. In Luke the hearing is not held until the next morning and Jesus is also in the courtyard (61). The fearful Peter follows "at a distance" as Jesus is led to the house of the high priest (54). Yet, his presence in the courtyard is an act of boldness! His body is there, "ready to go . . . to prison" with Jesus (33) but, in the presence of those who know otherwise, he denies even knowing Jesus! Only after his third denial, the crowing of the cock, and Jesus' looking at him, does Peter come back to his senses. Later he will be able to "turn back" (verse 32) and strengthen the other disciples.

Preparation: You may have many other things on your mind. But this powerful story calls for your undivided attention.

Read 22:54-62: The differing details of the four Gospel writers are fascinating, but for now let yourself enter into it as Luke tells it.

Reflection: Few of us have ever been tempted to deny being Jesus' followers, at least not like Peter was. But if we are honest, don't we deny Jesus every time we consciously make a choice that contradicts what we have learned from him? What about our assumptions about people of other racial or ethnic backgrounds? What about our support of war to resolve international differences? What about our ignoring of those who are hungry or homeless? What about our reluctance to visit those who are sick or in prison? What form does your denial take?

Prayer: Ask God to help you be more honest and courageous in your commitment to follow Jesus.

If you are the Messiah, tell us

Commentary: The hearing before the council opens with the demand, "If you are the Messiah, tell us." Having already decided that he was not, their real purpose was to find out if Jesus *claimed* to be the Messiah, which would constitute blasphemy and provide them with a possible case against him. But Jesus reminds them that even a direct answer would not make them believe. Then, alluding to Psalm 110:1, he points to his future place in the glory and power of God. When the council asks, "Are you, then, the Son of God?" Jesus makes them responsible for their own conclusion by answering, "You say that I am." Left without any legal ground to accuse him, they interpret his answer as self-incriminating and prepare to take him before Pilate. But they know that to convince the Roman governor to condemn him, the charge must involve more than a theological controversy among the Jews. Matthew and Mark imply that council members also participated in the mocking and beating of Jesus, but Luke says the guards alone were responsible.

Preparation: What feelings do you bring to praying scripture? Joy? Humility? Duty? Expectation? Faithfulness? Openness?

Read 22:63-71: The legal questions of the council are difficult to understand, as are Jesus' answers. If you have difficulty, look again at the commentary.

Reflection: Someone has said, "My mind is made up, don't confuse me with the facts." The minds of those on the high council were so closed that they had no interest in hearing what Jesus might have to say. They simply looked for any possible evidence to confirm what they had already decided was true. Thus their conclusion, "We don't need any witnesses" (22:71, TEV). Can you recall times when you or someone you know approached a religious or political question with this attitude?

Prayer: Pray that you might have the ability to hear the witness of others with an open mind and heart.

I find no reason to condemn this man

Commentary: The purpose of the hearing before the council was to find some way of accusing Jesus before the Roman authorities. When Jesus provided that reason by responding, "You say that I am" (the Messiah), the council quickly moved to take him before Pilate, the Roman governor. Once before Pilate, however, they expanded the charges to three: that he misled the people; that he urged the people not to pay taxes to the Emperor; and that he claimed to be the Messiah. Pilate, mindful of his responsibility to keep things peaceful, asked only about Jesus being "the king of the Jews." But Jesus' answer, "You say so," evoked from Pilate precisely the opposite response given to the same words by the high council! Pilate found no reason to condemn Jesus. Fearful that the opportunity to get rid of Jesus might be slipping through their hands, the council pressed its case even harder, adding the accusation that Jesus, a Galilean, was "starting a riot among the people all through Judea." As we will see in the next section, the information that Jesus was from Galilee provided Pilate with an excuse to shift the matter to another jurisdiction.

Preparation: Remember some struggles in your own life. Sometimes friends come through for us and sometimes they may abandon us. Only God is completely dependable.

Read 23:1-5: As you read this episode, imagine yourself as an objective observer watching the action from the sidelines.

Reflection: The first two charges brought against Jesus were clearly false, and the third was subject to interpretation. While most of us will never have the political or judicial power to decide such questions, we do hear accusations made against people we know. Such accusations are often based on rumors, personal grudges, or misunderstandings. The way we react to such accusations may well affect the life or reputation of other persons.

Prayer: Pray that you will always respond to accusations about other people with compassion, mercy, justice, and love.

He was hoping to see Jesus perform some miracle

Commentary: Pilate's motive for sending Jesus to Herod Antipas, who was also in town during the Passover Festival, is understandable. Surely he had no desire to make himself even less popular by condemning a man whose teaching had been enthusiastically received by the people. Still, the account of Jesus' being brought before Herod seems to serve no real purpose except perhaps to strengthen Luke's case against Roman culpability in the death of Jesus. The fact that it is reported only by Luke has caused some to question its historicity. If it really happened, why would Mark not have known about and reported it? Luke has already mentioned Herod's desire to see Jesus (9:9) and even his desire to kill him (13:31). But when the meeting actually occurred, Herod seemed content merely to question him, ask him to perform a miracle, and then make fun of him. Luke's final comment about this incident leading to the friendship of Herod and Pilate is unexplained. A few scholars have speculated that their former animosity could have been related, at least in part, to the incident reported by Luke in 13:1.

Preparation: How easy it is to avoid praying when we don't feel like it. But how often we are surprised by grace in those very prayer experiences we were reluctant to take time for!

Read 23:6-12: In your second reading of this account, try to get a sense of the character of Herod Antipas and your reaction to him.

Reflection: What were the motives behind Herod's questions and actions? Was he more relaxed now that Jesus was no longer in Galilee? Why do you think he wanted Jesus to "perform a miracle"? If he wanted to kill Jesus earlier (13:31), why, now that he had the opportunity, was he content to send him back to Pilate? If you had been a member of Herod's court with him in Jerusalem, what advice would you have given him about Jesus?

Prayer: Pray for a better understanding of your own mixed feelings about Jesus.

He has done nothing to deserve death

Commentary: Now, with Jesus before him again, Pilate declares three more times in the presence of the people that he finds no reason for condemnation, "and neither has Herod." Some have suggested that this is Luke's attempt to relieve some of the tension between Rome and the early church over the question of responsibility for Jesus' death. Luke offers no explanation for the sudden anger of the crowd, even though Mark says the chief priests stirred up the crowd to ask for the release of Barabbas instead of Jesus. The custom of releasing a prisoner at the time of the Passover Festival is not found in many early manuscripts of Luke and is thus explained in a footnote to verse 16. That custom provided Pilate with an excuse for yielding to the angry crowd rather than following his own judgment about Jesus' innocence. Luke also omits Jesus' mocking by Pilate's soldiers. It is ironic that Jesus, who is innocent of the charge of insurrection, is condemned, while Barabbas, guilty of the same crime, is released.

Preparation: Have you looked up at the stars on a dark night, away from the distracting lights of the city? Recall that experience and what you felt, as you get ready to pray.

Read 23:13-25: Try to dismiss the details provided by the other Gospels in order to to hear the full impact of Luke's account.

Reflection: It is easy to sympathize with Pilate, especially in the Lucan account. He is apparently caught between his obligation to administer justice and his responsibility to maintain order in a crowded city at festival time. He understands the motives of the religious leaders but finds no truth to the charges they have made. He seems to have no choice other than to go along with the demands of an ugly crowd. But is this really true? What might you have done, had you been in Pilate's position?

Prayer: Pray for all in positions of power who are faced with making decisions on difficult questions, and for yourself when you are tempted to take the easy way out.

As they led him away . . .

Commentary: Luke has adapted Mark's account of Jesus being led to the place of crucifixion in order to focus on the people along the way and their response to what was happening. By adding the detail that Simon of Cyrene carried the cross *behind* Jesus, Luke makes Simon an example for all who would follow Jesus by taking up the cross. When Luke says, "A great number of the people followed him" (27), he may be suggesting "the reappearance of those common people who daily listened to Jesus in the temple."[70] Among them were women who were weeping for Jesus. It is to these that Jesus addresses an extended word of warning about the fate of Jerusalem (28-31), concluding with a proverb comparing the burning qualities of green wood and dry wood. If such a thing can happen to the green wood (the innocent Jesus), how much more will be the tragedy of the dry wood (the unbelieving Jerusalem).

Preparation: If you have ever driven from the city to a favorite place in the country you know the feeling of emerging from your car to discover the quietness and the clean country air. Recall such a moment as you get ready to pray.

Read 23:26-32: As you read and pray, allow yourself to envision the people Luke describes "as they led him away."

Reflection: Can you think of tragic events in our own time that point to even greater tragedy in the future because we don't take them seriously today? What events or conditions can you think of that are like "green wood" compared to the "dry wood" events that may follow? Is our disregard for the environment like green wood? What about our neglect of systemic problems that seem to cause rather than alleviate poverty? What about our nation's continuing sale of arms in the post-cold war era? What things in your personal life are like green wood now?

Prayer: Ask God to help you to fully appreciate the relationship between today's green wood and tomorrow's dry wood.

Jesus, remember me when you enter upon your reign

Commentary: The crucifixion of Jesus is probably the most common subject in the history of Christian art. Yet it is not even described by Luke, who simply says, "When they came to the place that is called The Skull, they crucified Jesus there with the criminals, one on his right and one on his left." The rest of the account is devoted to the actions and taunts of others and to the remarkable exchange between Jesus and the two criminals, found only in Luke. In verse 35 Luke once again distinguishes between the people who watch quietly and their leaders who scoff at Jesus. The words of 34a, "Father, forgive them; for they do not know what they are doing," are apparently addressed to the Jewish leaders and to the Romans. The fact that these words are not found in the earliest manuscripts and seem to interrupt the flow of the text would suggest that they were a later addition to the Gospel. The division of Jesus' clothing in 34b is seen as a fulfillment of Psalm 22:18. Finally, Jesus is three times taunted to save himself (by the leaders, the soldiers, and the criminals). He continues his saving ministry, even on the cross, but it is the repentant criminal that he saves, not himself.

Preparation: Try using the "Jesus prayer" as your way of centering: "Lord Jesus Christ, have mercy on me, a sinner."

Read 23:33-43: Listen to the different voices heard in this reading.

Reflection: Listen to the scoffing of the religious leaders: "He saved others; let him save himself if he is the Messiah . . . "
Listen to the soldiers, offering him cheap wine: "If you are the King of the Jews, save yourself!"
Listen to the first criminal deriding Jesus: "Are you not the Messiah? Save yourself and us!"
Now, listen to the other criminal: "Jesus, remember me when you come into your kingdom."

Prayer: Can you make the prayer of the second criminal your prayer?

Surely this was an innocent man

Commentary: Luke's passion narrative culminates with a surprisingly brief account of Jesus' death. In six verses he reports two cosmic signs (darkness and the tearing of the curtain in the Temple), Jesus' final prayer, his death, and the reactions of those present. The language about darkness and the tearing of the curtain in the Temple sounds apocalyptic, but as Fitzmyer suggests, "should rather be related to the Lucan idea of evil's 'hour' and the 'power of darkness' (22:53), which reign as Jesus dies."[71] Jesus' death is reported in a single verse with his final prayer, drawn from Psalm 31:5. The last three verses are devoted to the reactions of: a Roman soldier, the gathered crowds, and "all those who knew Jesus personally" (TEV). The crowds respond with signs of penitence, and the soldier becomes yet another Roman witness to the innocence of Jesus. Luke does not report the desertion of the disciples at the time of Jesus' arrest. Perhaps some of them were among those he now mentions who "were standing at a distance watching everything"(49). Also present were the women who had followed him from Galilee, three of whom have already been identified (8:1-3) and will shortly be named again as the first witnesses to the resurrection.

Preparation: If you know the spiritual, "Were you there when they crucified my Lord," read or sing it as you center yourself.

Read 23:44-49: During your second reading, pause for a time of reflection after each of the six verses.

Reflection: In Mark the response of the Roman soldier is, "Truly this man was God's Son!" (NRSV). Luke, either drawing on another source or adapting the words for his own purposes (see commentary on 23:13-25) has, "Surely this was an innocent man." In either case it is a witness to the power of redemptive suffering, especially if the soldier was among those who had mocked Jesus.

Prayer: Pray that your own witness to Jesus will always be a witness to the power of redemptive suffering.

There was a good and righteous man named Joseph . . .

Commentary: Luke ends his passion narrative with a brief account of Jesus' burial. Again, he has eliminated a number of Mark's details. There is no mention of Pilate's making sure of Jesus' death before granting Joseph of Arimathea permission to bury him. We hear nothing of Joseph's boldness or his role in the hearing, except that he was a member of the council who disagreed with the plot against Jesus. He is described as "a good and righteous man," recalling the description of Zechariah, Elizabeth, and Simeon in Luke's birth narrative. His placing the body in "a tomb where no one had ever been laid," is reminiscent of Jesus' entering Jerusalem on, "a colt that has never been ridden" (19:30). Not mentioned are the purchase of the linen cloth or the sealing of the tomb (Mark 15:46). Nor does Luke name the women who witnessed the burial, even though he adds the detail about their returning home to prepare the spices and ointments. Long before the Gospels were written, the burial of Jesus was considered an important part of Christian preaching. For the modern church it serves as a reminder that there can be no Easter rejoicing apart from the painful reality of Good Friday.

Preparation: As a way to center, sing or repeat: "Were you there when they laid him in the tomb?"

Read 23:50-56: Pause to recall some of the events in the twenty-four hours beginning with the Passover meal in the upper room.

Reflection: Take time to imagine what some of the other persons we have met in the passion story might have been feeling and doing on that Friday evening, as Joseph of Arimathea and the women went to the tomb with Jesus' body—the Roman soldier at the foot of the cross, the High Priest, Pilate, Herod, Simon of Cyrene, Peter, and Barabbas.

Prayer: Pray for all Christians everywhere, that the story of the passion may continue to capture our imagination and call us to "good and righteous" lives.

THE RESURRECTION NARRATIVE
Luke 24:1-53

Why are you looking among the dead for one who is alive? He is not
here; he has been raised.
(Luke 24:5b-6a, TEV)

THE BIOGRAPHIES OF THE GREAT AND FAMOUS very often conclude
with an account of their death and burial. But the Gospels are
much more than biographies, and Jesus is much more than a
great and famous person. The climax of the passion is not death
but the overcoming of death. Indeed, one of the unique
characteristics of a Gospel as a literary form is the fact that the
entire story is told in the light of the resurrection. It is not a
"surprise ending," but something the reader knows from the
beginning. Even so, the resurrection story has the power to
surprise and amaze us with every reading.

Luke's resurrection narrative is in four parts: the
discovery of the empty tomb (1-12); the appearance of Jesus to
two followers on the road to Emmaus (13-35); his appearance to
the disciples and others in Jerusalem (36-49); and his final
blessing and ascension (50-53).

In Luke, unlike the other Gospels, all of Jesus' resurrection
appearances take place in the vicinity of Jerusalem and on the
first day. Galilee is mentioned by the two men encountered at the
tomb (verse 6), but there is no reminder, as in Mark and Matthew,
that Jesus will meet his disciples there. Even so, Luke says in his
preface to Acts that, "For forty days after his death he appeared
to them many times in ways that proved beyond doubt that he
was alive" (Acts 1:3a, TEV).

The final two verses (52-53) are unique to this Gospel.
Luke tells us that the followers of Jesus returned to Jerusalem
after the ascension near Bethany, "and spent all their time in the
Temple giving thanks to God." Thus he ends his Gospel in the
Temple where it began in chapter 1 with the annunciation to
Zechariah.

Why are you looking among the dead for one who is alive?

Commentary: The four empty tomb accounts, critically compared, may present more questions than answers! Which women, other than Mary Magdalene, were at the tomb? Did they arrive at sunrise as in Matthew and Mark or in the dark as in John? Did they encounter one or two men or angels? Were they instructed to tell the disciples or not? Did Peter go to the tomb alone or with John? Only Luke assumes that that the women at the tomb had been present when Jesus predicted his death and resurrection in Galilee (24:6 and 9:22). Is this his way of saying that they were among Jesus' closest disciples? Craddock suggests that the presence of *two* men at the tomb may be Luke's way of joining this story to the transfiguration (9:30) and the ascension (Acts 1:9-11), inviting us to see all three as one category of experience.[72] In any case it is Jesus' later appearance to the disciples that provides evidence for the resurrection, not the empty tomb. The absence of his body is merely a source of fear and amazement (5 and 12).

Preparation: Let go of the "blended" story your mind knows from all four Gospels, and hear it now as Luke tells it.

Read 24:1-12: Read the empty tomb story as if for the first time.

Reflection: We *expect* Jesus to appeal to the masses, but he concentrates on a few disciples. We *expect* him to be a king, but he takes the role of a servant. We *expect* him to be hard on sinners, but he invites himself to their homes for dinner! We *expect* him to hold traditional male values, but he is radically open to the needs of women. We *expect* him to honor family values, but he causes conflict in families. We *expect* him to be gentle and nonviolent, but he trashes the Temple courtyard and screams at the Pharisees. We *expect* him to defend himself, but he stands silently at his own trial. We *expect* to find his body in the tomb, but. . . .

Prayer: Pray that you might be more and more open to the *unexpected*, upside-down values of God's reign.

Then their eyes were opened, and they recognized him

Commentary: The story of the walk to Emmaus is one of Luke's finest contributions to the Gospel. The setting is a brief journey of two disciples, which begins and ends in Jerusalem. In it Luke offers his readers an appearance of the resurrected Jesus; a summary of the gospel (18-24); and a eucharistic meal in which two disciples finally understand who Jesus is. Some have pointed to the striking structural parallel between this story and Luke's story of the Ethiopian eunuch in Acts 8:26-40. Eugene LaVerdiere sees the Emmaus story framed by the disciples' failure to recognize Jesus (16) and their finally recognizing him (31). Within that frame are a dialogue narrative on the way to Emmaus (17-27) and a meal narrative in the home of the disciples (28-30).[73] Jesus the invited guest (29) becomes Jesus the host (30) as he takes, blesses, breaks, and gives the bread. These actions, reflecting the feeding of the multitude (9:16) and the Last Supper (22:19), were already familiar in the eucharistic meals of the church in Luke's time. With the scriptures interpreted to them on the road and Jesus "made known to them in the breaking of bread," Cleopas and his companion return at once to Jerusalem to share the news with the eleven disciples and the others gathered with them.

Preparation: Recall the journey you have been on as you have prayed the Gospel According to Luke.

Read 24:13-35: Take plenty of time as you read this story. Pause frequently to appreciate all that is to be found in it.

Reflection: How often do we fail to see with our hearts what we can see with our eyes? The inability of the two disciples to recognize Jesus on the road was a spiritual problem, not a physical one. It is more than ironic that when he was "made known to them in the breaking of bread," they could no longer see him with their eyes. To see or not to see, that is the question.

Prayer: Ask God to help you understand that, "What is essential is invisible to the eye."[74]

LUKE 24:36-49 (NRSV)

He opened their minds to understand the scriptures

Commentary: Luke does not identify the "companions" who were gathered with "the eleven" in Jerusalem. But they probably included the women from Galilee (23:49), Jesus' mother and brothers (Acts 1:14), and perhaps others as well. The place was likely the same upper room where they had gathered just three nights earlier to celebrate the Passover meal (see Acts 1:12-13). Now, as Cleopas and his companion tell about what happened to them on the road to Emmaus, Jesus suddenly appears among them. Verses 36-43 are structured much like the Emmaus story: Jesus appears, is not recognized, chides them for their doubts, interprets the scriptures to them, and shares their food; they respond with joy. But here the emphasis is on his physical, rather than his spiritual presence. The disciples are instructed to continue preaching repentance and forgiveness in Jesus' name to all nations, beginning in Jerusalem. Finally, they are told to remain in Jerusalem until the power of the Spirit comes to them.

Preparation: As Jesus was present to those in Jerusalem, allow him to be present to you, "opening your mind to the scriptures."

Read 24:36-49: Pause for a few moments of reflection after verse 43. Then go on to the second part of the reading.

Reflection: Can you imagine the emotional and spiritual state of "the disciples and their companions"? Their day had begun very early in the morning when the women rushed back with the news about the empty tomb. Then Peter, having gone to see for himself, confirmed what the others had dismissed as "nonsense" (TEV). Still, no one really understood what had happened. As Luke says, ". . . in their joy they were disbelieving and still wondering" (24:41). Perhaps their minds and hearts were not finally opened to understand until the ascension or even the Pentecost event. Has praying the scripture helped to open your mind and heart?

Prayer: Pray that you will grow in your own understanding of the scriptures as you continue to pray them.

They were continually in the temple blessing God

Commentary: That Luke contradicts the time and place of the ascension in Acts 1:1-12 is not a problem. He may have purposely compressed the events of his Gospel account into a single day for brevity and dramatic effect. In either case the disciples would have returned "from the Mount of Olives," since it was on the road to Bethany. It should be noted that not all early manuscripts include the words, "and was carried up into heaven." The gravitational implications of the ascension are secondary to its theological meaning, which addresses the glorification of the risen and victorious Christ. Such glory may be seen not only in the image of Christ seated "at the right hand of God," but in the dramatic change in the disciples themselves. No longer "disbelieving and . . . wondering" (41) they returned with great joy and "were continually in the Temple blessing God," as they waited for the promised coming of the Holy Spirit. Luke's Gospel ends, where it began, in the Temple at the time of worship.

Preparation:

> Prayer is the soul's sincere desire, unuttered or expressed,
> the motion of a hidden fire that trembles in the breast.[75]

Read 24:50-53: Imagine standing with the disciples as Jesus gives you his final blessing . . . and disappears from your sight.

Reflection:

> Let the same mind be in you that was in Christ Jesus, who, though he was in the form of God, did not regard equality with God as something to be exploited, but emptied himself, taking the form of a slave, being born in human likeness. And being found in human form, he humbled himself and became obedient to the point of death—even death on a cross. Therefore God also highly exalted him and gave him the name that is above every name, so that at the name of Jesus every knee should bend, in heaven and on earth and under the earth, and every tongue should confess that Jesus Christ is Lord, to the glory of God the Father.
> (Philippians 2:5-11, NRSV)

Prayer:

> *Now, Lord, you have kept your promise, and you may let your servant go in peace. With my own eyes I have seen your salvation, which you have prepared in the presence of all peoples: A light to reveal your will to the Gentiles and bring glory to your people Israel.*
>
> (Luke 2:29-32, TEV)

♦ ♦ ♦

> *Dear Theophilus:*
> *In my first book I wrote about all the things that Jesus did and taught from the time he began his work until the day he was taken up to heaven. Before he was taken up, he gave instructions by the power of the Holy Spirit to the men he had chosen as his apostles. For forty days after his death he appeared to them many times in ways that proved beyond doubt that he was alive. They saw him, and he talked with them about the Kingdom of God. And when they came together, he gave them this order: "Do not leave Jerusalem, but wait for the gift I told you about, the gift my Father promised. John baptized with water, but in a few days you will be baptized with the Holy Spirit."*
>
> (Acts 1:1-5, TEV)

[216]

NOTES

Praying Scripture

[1] American Bible Society, bookmark, "10th Annual Worldwide Bible Reading," 1953.

[2] As quoted in *The Art of Prayer: An Orthodox Anthology,* ed. by Timothy Ware, (London: Faber and Faber, 1966), 110.

[3] Nouwen, Henri J.M., *The Way of the Heart,* (New York: Seabury, 1981) 76.

[4] Merton, Thomas, trans., *The Wisdom of the Desert,* (New York: New Directions, 1960) 20.

[5] Keating, Thomas, *The Heart of the World: A Spiritual Catechism,* (New York: Crossroad, 1981) 48.

[6] Kelly, Thomas R., *A Testament of Devotion,* (New York: Harper & Bros, 1941) 29.

[7] LeShan, Lawrence, *How to Meditate,* (New York: Bantam Books, 1975) 14.

An Invitation to Luke's Gospel

[8] Baird, William, *The Interpreter's One Volume Commentary on the Bible,* 672.

[9] Fitzmyer, Joseph A., *The Gospel According to Luke,* 42.

[10] LaVerdiere, Eugene, *Luke, xv.*

[11] Johnson, Luke Timothy, *The Gospel of Luke,* 10.

[12] Johnson, 8.

[13] Baird, 672

[14] Kodell, Jerome, *The Gospel According to Luke,* 7.

[15] LaVerdiere, *xxii.*

[16] Craddock, Fred B., *Luke,* 8.

[17] Craddock, 9.

[18] LaVerdiere, *xi.*

[19] Schaberg, Jane, "Luke," *The Women's Bible Commentary,* 275.

[20] Schaberg, 275.

[21] Schaberg, 277.

[22] Schaberg, 289.

[23] Schaberg, 291.

[24] Schaberg, 275.

[25] Schaberg, 284f.

[26] Schaberg, 281.

[27] Schaberg, 282.
[28] Schaberg, 291.

Using the Meditations in Groups

[29] van den Heuvel, Cor, *The Haiku Anthology*, 249.

Meditations

[30] Kodell, Jerome, *The Gospel According to Luke*, 12.
[31] Kodell, 13.
[32] LaVerdiere, Eugene, 53
[33] Craddock, 66.
[34] Gundry, Robert H., Matthew: *A Commentary on His Literary and Theological Art.* (Eerdmans, 1982), 68 (as quoted in *Pulpit Resource*, Vol. 15, No. 4, October-December 1987).
[35] Kodell, 39.
[36] Craddock, 93.
[37] Harvey, A. E., *Companion to the New Testament*, 244.
[38] Dodd, C. H., *The Parables of the Kingdom*, 16 (quoted in Craddock, 108).
[39] Craddock, 117f.
[40] Harvey, 250.
[41] Kodell, 58.
[42] Paraphrased from: Merton, Thomas, *The Wisdom of the Desert*, 36f.
[43] Craddock, 160.
[44] Luther, Martin, verse from his hymn, "A Mighty Fortress Is Our God."
[45] Tolstoy, Leo, story told in *Homiletics*, July-September 1989, 20.
[46] Fosdick, Harry Emerson, "God of Grace and God of Glory" (verse 3).
[47] LaVerdiere, 178.
[48] Donders, Joseph G., *Praying and Preaching the Sunday Gospel*, 182.
[49] Kodell, 72.
[50] Karris, Robert J., *Invitation to Luke*, 175.
[51] Craddock, 178
[52] LaVerdiere, 197.
[53] Craddock, 182.
[54] LaVerdiere, 199.
[55] Fitzmyer, 1087.
[56] Fitzmyer, 1088.
[57] Craddock, 188.
[58] See Fitzmyer, p 1097ff, for a discussion of this question.
[59] Craddock, 199.

[60] Craddock, 200.
[61] Craddock, 209.
[62] Fitzmyer, 1208.
[63] Talbert, Charles H., *Reading Luke*, 178.
[64] Craddock, 225.
[65] Fitzmyer, 1255.
[66] LaVerdiere, 246.
[67] Fitzmyer, 1386.
[68] Caird, G. B., *The Gospel of St. Luke*, 237 (quoted on p. 1386 of
     Fitzmyer)
[69] Kelly, Thomas R., 29.
[70] Craddock, 271.
[71] Fitzmyer, 1519.
[72] Craddock, 281f.
[73] LaVerdiere, 284f.
[74] de Saint-Exupery, Antoine, *The Little Prince*, 70.
[75] Montgomery, James, "Prayer is the Soul's Sincere Desire," (verse 1).

A SELECTED BIBLIOGRAPHY

Barclay, William. *The Gospel of Luke.* Rev. ed. Philadelphia: The Westminster Press, 1975.

Craddock, Fred B. *Luke.* Interpretation: Bible Commentary for Teaching and Preaching. Louisville, KY: John Knox Press, 1990.

Dodd, C. H. *The Parables of the Kingdom.* Rev. ed. New York: Charles Scribner's Sons, 1961.

Donders, Joseph G. *Praying and Preaching the Sunday Gospel.* Maryknoll, NY: Orbis Books, 1988.

Fitzmyer, Joseph A. *The Gospel According to Luke.* 2 vols. The Anchor Bible. Garden City, NY: Doubleday, 1981, 1985.

Gundry, Robert H. *Matthew: A Commentary on His Literary and Theological Art.* Grand Rapids, MI: W. B. Eerdmans Pub., 1982.

Harvey, A. E. *Companion to the New Testament.* Oxford: Oxford University Press, Cambridge University Press, 1970.

Johnson, Luke Timothy. *The Gospel of Luke.* Sacra Pagina Series, vol. 3. Collegeville, MN: The Liturgical Press, 1991.

Karris, Robert J. *Invitation to Luke.* Garden City, NY: Image Books, 1977.

Keating, Thomas. *The Heart of the World: A Spiritual Catechism.* New York: Crossroad, 1981.

Kelly, Thomas R. *A Testament of Devotion.* New York: Harper & Brothers, 1941.

Kodell, Jerome. *The Gospel According to Luke.* Collegeville Bible Commentary. Collegeville, MN: The Liturgical Press, 1983.

LaVerdiere, Eugene. *Luke.* New Testament Message, vol. 5. Collegeville, MN: The Liturgical Press, 1990.

LeShan, Lawrence. *How to Meditate*. New York: Bantam Books, 1975.

Maloney, George A. *Prayer of the Heart*. Notre Dame, IN: Ave Maria Press, 1981.

Merton, Thomas, trans. *The Wisdom of the Desert*. New York: New Directions, 1960.

Newsome, Carol A. and Sharon H. Ringe, eds. *The Women's Bible Commentary*. Louisville, KY: Westminster/John Knox Press, 1992.

Nomura, Yushi. *Desert Wisdom: Sayings From the Desert Fathers*. New York: Doubleday, 1984.

Nouwen, Henri J. M. *The Way of the Heart*. New York: The Seabury Press, 1981.

Pennington, M. Basil. *A Place Apart*. Garden City, NY: Doubleday, 1983.

Pennington, M. Basil. *Centering Prayer*. Garden City, NY: Doubleday, 1980.

Russell, Norman, trans. *The Lives of the Desert Fathers*. London: Mowbray, 1980.

Stewart, Columba. *The World of the Desert Fathers*. Oxford: SLG Press, 1986.

Talbert, Charles H. *Reading Luke: A Literary and Theological Commentary on the Third Gospel*. New York: Crossroad, 1992.

Van den Heuvel, Cor, comp. *The Haiku Anthology*. Garden City, NY: Anchor Press, 1974.

Ward, Benedicta, trans. *The Sayings of the Desert Fathers*. London: Mowbray, 1975.

Ward, Benedicta, trans. *The Wisdom of the Desert Fathers*. Oxford: SLG Press, 1975.

INDEX OF THEMES

Accountability
    12:41-48; 13:6-9; 16:1-13; 17:1-4; 17:7-10; 19:11-27; 20:9-18;
    22:39-46; 22:47-53; 23:13-25; 23:26-38
Amazement
    2:15-21; 2:22-35; 2:39-52; 4:31-37; 5:1-11; 5:17-26; 8:22-25;
    9:37-43a; 11:14-23
Angels
    1:5-22; 2:8-15; 2:15-20; 4:1-13; 12:8-12; 24:1-12
Anger (bitterness, etc.)
    12:57-59
Annunciation
    1:5-22; 1:26-38
Anxiety
    12:22-31; 12:32-34
Apocalyptic themes
    21:5-19; 21:20-24; 21:34-38
Ascension
    24:50-53
Asking
    11:5-13; 18:35-43
Authority
    4:31-37; 9:1-6; 10:21-24; 11:14-23; 11:29-32; 13:10-17; 20:1-8;
    23:13-25
Baptism
    3:1-20; 3:21-22; 7:18-35; 12:49-53
Beatitudes
    6:20-26
Blessing
    24:50-53
Bread
    4:1-13; 9:10-17; 22:14-23; 24:13-35
Burial of Jesus
    23:50-56
Calling of Disciples
    5:1-11; 5:27-32; 6:12-16; 14:25-33

Caring
    10:25-37; 13:6-9; 14:1-6; 14:12-14; 15:1-2; 16:19-31
Children
    9:46-48; 18:15-17
Commitment
    12:4-7; 12:49-53; 13:22-30; 14:15-24; 14:25-33; 14:34-35; 18:18-30; 19:11-27; 22:31-34
Community
    14:1-6; 15:1-2; 17:1-4; 24:36-49
Compassion
    10:25-37; 14:1-6; 14:12-14; 15:1-2; 15:11-32; 16:19-31; 23:33-43
Confession
    14:25-33; 18:9-14; 19:1-10; 19:41-44; 22:47-53; 22:63-71; 23:33-43
Conflict
    12:49-53; 12:57-59; 13:10-17; 17:1-4; 20:1-8; 20:19-26; 22:35-38; 22:47-53; 23:1-5; 23:6-12; 23:33-43
Darkness
    11:33-36; 22:1-6; 22:47-53; 22:54-62; 23:44-49
Death
    22:1-6; 23:44-49; 23:50-56; 24:1-12
Demons
    4:31-37; 4:38-41; 8:1-3; 8:26-39; 9:49-50; 10:17-20; 11:14-23; 11:24-26
Denial
    22:54-62; 23:26-38
Desert Spirituality
    3:1-21; 4:1-13
Devil (see Satan)
Discipleship
    8:1-3; 9:46-48; 9:57-62; 10:1-12; 12:32-34; 12:49-53; 12:54-56; 13:22-30; 14:1-6; 14:15-24; 14:25-33; 14:34-35; 16:14-18; 17:7-10; 18:18-30; 19:11-27; 22:39-46; 24:36-49
Disgrace
    1:23-25; 15:11-32
Enemies
    6:27-38
Enthusiasm
    12:54-56: 14:25-33; 14:34-35; 19:28-40; 22:31-34
Eternal life

ABOUT THE AUTHOR

The Reverend Don Collins is a United Methodist pastor and has served the Church of the Good Hope in Milwaukee, Wisconsin, since 1987. Prior to that he was a campus minister for more than twenty years and a past president of the National Campus Ministry Association.

Reverend Collins is a native of Colorado and is a graduate of the University of Denver and the Iliff School of Theology in Denver. His professional interests include liturgical renewal, spiritual formation, and ecumenism. He is the author of *Like Trees That Grow Beside a Stream: Praying through the Psalms,* published by Upper Room Books in 1991.

Since he was in high school, Don's favorite hobby has been genealogy. He is the author of a family history, *The Mabry Family,* published in 1987. He and his wife, Edith McFadden Collins, are interested in national and international issues and both have held local elected offices. They have three married children.